The EVERYTHING
Home Decorating Book

Dear Reader:

My husband and I bought a house in the country several years ago. It's a modest Cape-style home built in the early 1800s. I suspect the dining room walls were never sunshine yellow above the bright white wainscoting before, but they are now.

The decorating plans we have for this house are to make it comfortable for us. Not for houseguests or the next generation—for us, living here, right now. Oh sure, we'll give a nod to the rich history of this sturdy home, and we do our best to accommodate guests despite its small size. But we both work from our home. We spend a lot of time here and use it hard, and it needs to work for us.

The Everything® Home Decorating Book will set you off on a journey to make your own home yours, too. The hardest part about writing this book has been to keep writing instead of using the inspiration it has given me, setting the writing aside, and working on decorating projects of my own!

Enjoy the book and enjoy decorating your home, whether "home" is a one-room efficiency apartment or a twenty-four-room mansion.

Cheryl Kimball

The EVERYTHING® Series

Editorial

Publishing Director	Gary M. Krebs
Managing Editor	Kate McBride
Copy Chief	Laura MacLaughlin
Acquisitions Editor	Bethany Brown
Development Editor	Karen Johnson Jacot
Production Editor	Khrysti Nazzaro

Production

Production Director	Susan Beale
Production Manager	Michelle Roy Kelly
Series Designers	Daria Perreault
	Colleen Cunningham
Cover Design	Paul Beatrice
	Frank Rivera
Layout and Graphics	Colleen Cunningham
	Rachael Eiben
	Michelle Roy Kelly
	Daria Perreault
	Erin Ring
Series Cover Artist	Barry Littmann
Interior Photography	©Corel—Residential Interiors
Color Insert Photography	Elizabeth Whiting & Associates
Illustration of Ba-Gua Energy Map	Kathie Kelleher

THE
EVERYTHING®
HOME DECORATING BOOK

A room-by-room guide to
making your home beautiful

Cheryl Kimball

Adams Media Corporation
Avon, Massachusetts

An Everything® Series Book.
Everything® and everything.com® are registered trademarks of F+W Publications, Inc.

Published by Adams Media, an F+W Publications Company
57 Littlefield Street, Avon, MA 02322 U.S.A.
www.adamsmedia.com

ISBN: 1-58062-885-0
Printed in the United States of America.

J I H G F E D C

Library of Congress Cataloging-in-Publication Data
Kimball, Cheryl.
The everything home decorating book / Cheryl Kimball.
p.   cm.   (An everything series book)
ISBN 1-58062-885-0
1. Interior decoration–Amateurs' manuals. I. Title. II. Series:
Everything series.
NK2115.K488   2003
747—dc21   2003001929

This publication is designed to provide accurate and authoritative information with regard to the subject matter covered. It is sold with the understanding that the publisher is not engaged in rendering legal, accounting, or other professional advice. If legal advice or other expert assistance is required, the services of a competent professional person should be sought.
—From a *Declaration of Principles* jointly adopted by a Committee of the American Bar Association and a Committee of Publishers and Associations

Many of the designations used by manufacturers and sellers to distinguish their products are claimed as trademarks. Where those designations appear in this book and Adams Media was aware of a trademark claim, the designations have been printed with initial capital letters.

This book is available at quantity discounts for bulk purchases.
For information, call 1-800-872-5627.

Contents

Top Ten Ways
to Spruce Up Your Home Décor

1. Make simple curtains from pieces of fabric. Cut a neat edge on either end and drape the fabric in half over a curtain rod.

2. Paint the walls a cheery or fun new color for a quick way to freshen up any room.

3. Decorate with things that you use, like cookbooks in the kitchen, a wine rack in the dining room, a clock. Find things that serve dual purpose, like bookends that hold bottles of wine.

4. Use feng shui to rearrange your furniture to increase your well-being, wealth, and happiness.

5. Buy frames inexpensively at the home section of any department store and frame nice greeting cards.

6. If you have a small patch of dirt outside your home, throw a few flower seeds in the ground in the spring and grow your own decorations. Pitchers can be bought inexpensively at "antique" shops and make great, interesting vases.

7. Take some free classes at do-it-yourself home stores to learn how to do simple projects yourself instead of hiring someone.

8. Buy a bulletin board or some cork squares and create an ever-changing wall of personal photos.

9. Cover plain outlet and light switchplates with striking contact paper.

10. Simply move furniture, lights, and art around in a room (or room to room) once in a while.

Introduction

▶HOME DECORATING IS A PASTIME that stretches through the centuries. The ancient Egyptians took it to their graves, decorating mausoleums with all the comforts of home so they could enjoy their belongings and be comfortable in the next life.

Most of us think it's hard enough to find the time to make our homes comfortable in this life! But once you get hooked on home decorating, you will be hooked for good.

Decorating is a great combination of practicality and frivolity. It is possible to combine both effectively, so that a room takes on a life of its own. Arrange the furniture for the practical use of the room, then sneak in some whimsical accessories—from throw-pillow fabrics with a funky design to a framed postcard of a dog on a donkey—and you get both comfort and a smile.

Plan your decorating carefully, but not so carefully that your rooms look like museums. Houses are well used. They are built to stand up to the lifestyle of their occupants, and they should be decorated in that spirit as well.

If you get really interested in decorating, there are even university programs and courses through museums that can teach you more about the decorative arts. But for now, let's explore the many facets that home decorating has to offer that you can put to immediate practical use in your own home. Ⓔ

Chapter 1

Decorating, Remodeling, Renovating, Restoring

Decorating your home is a fun and creative pursuit, whether the sky's the limit or you are on a tight budget. But decorating isn't the only change a home can go through. Just what are the main types of home refurbishing that are possible, and how do they differ from each other?

Personal Expression

Your home, whether it's a small apartment in the city or a huge country estate, is second only to your clothing as your most personal form of expression. There are many ways, large and small, that you can use that canvas.

Some ways, like restoration, can take vast amounts of expertise, time, and funding. But home decoration is something anyone can do—and you do it almost every day whether you call it decorating or not! Move a chair, hang a mirror, change the table linens, and you're decorating.

Planned decorating is a little more precise than the random changes you make on a regular basis. You may choose to remodel, renovate, or redecorate any room in the house, or even the whole house!

Restoring a Vintage House

When you restore a home, you take it back to its original form. Restoration usually falls on the charts as the most expensive type of home project. It also takes a certain amount of expertise; if you don't have the expertise and don't have the time to acquire it, you'll need to hire a professional.

Getting It Right

A home doesn't have to be hundreds of years old to be a restoration project. Suppose you buy a 1950s Sears house—yes, the Sears that we know today used to sell houses from their catalog. The house has probably been remodeled over the years to match the style of the decade and to suit the different needs of the different families who lived there.

But Sears houses were quite lovely, often in Craftsman style with a lot of built-ins and wood details, and restoring them to their original appearance both inside and out became a fashionable thing to do. Perhaps you would like to restore yours to what it would have looked like when the pieces were first put together back in 1954. This may entail extensive work like tearing down an addition on the back, or it may mean smaller things like removing the plywood knickknack shelf covering the decorative stained glass window above the front door. Shag carpets may cover wood floors in the living room and dining room; once revealed, the wood floors may still be in great shape and just need some loving care.

All of this takes some upfront research to understand just how the house would have looked when it was originally built. Your research would include locating and touring some Sears houses of the same vintage as your house that haven't been extensively remodeled. You can probably get your hands on a Sears catalog that featured your home, and at least one book has been written on these American icons. When you are done with your restoration project, you will have a Sears home that fundamentally resembles its catalog description.

FACT

In the 1970s when the restoration era was gaining popularity, a magazine called *Old House Journal* began to offer information and advice to homeowners who were interested in restoring their homes. One part of their magazine that has remained extremely popular is a column called "Remuddling." Each month the remuddling column features a picture of a house as it looks today next to either a picture of the house as it looked in its original form or an un-remuddled house similar in style in the same neighborhood. Look for *Old House Journal* on well-stocked newsstands or check out their great Web site at *www.oldhousejournal.com*.

Making It Modern

Pure restoration doesn't mean you can't have the advantages of contemporary appliances and furniture. In fact, part of the fun and challenge is choosing modern things that fit the basic feel of the restored home. Restoration has become popular enough that manufacturers began to meet the needs of these particular consumers. For instance, a few kitchen appliance companies have designed their appliances so that they can be covered with wood fronts. This helps them blend into the wood cabinetry, letting your kitchen look more like it comes from the era in which it was originally built while still allowing you to enjoy modern and efficient conveniences.

Chances are that if you are renting, you are not going to spend time and money on a restoration project. In fact, your landlord may not let you even if you were willing. But renting a vintage home can often give you a sense of whether or not it is the style of home you would like to purchase and take on as a restoration project.

Restoring an older home is not something for the faint of heart, but it is an admirable undertaking for those who enjoy challenges.

Renovating a House

A renovation project is usually less extensive than restoration and perhaps a little more complex than remodeling. Renovation often takes the form of significant repair work to a house. Renovation is chosen over restoration, generally speaking, in cases where the house may not have the historical significance to make it a restoration project or where the house may be historically of interest but needs work, not because it has been altered but because it is deteriorating.

What Is Involved?

Renovation can be extremely expensive and may consist of gutting an entire home down to its rafters and sills, or it may be simpler with a focus on just one room. The most common one-room renovation is the kitchen and the bathroom. The renovation of these rooms can only be categorized as "major" since they are complicated with electrical and plumbing work and appliances and fixtures that often need substantial updating if not out-and-out replacement. Minor renovation to a less complex room like a living room may include rewiring for modern electronic equipment, removing old and installing new wall-to-wall carpeting, and opening up a pass-through to the kitchen to create a more contemporary, open feel.

The more complex rooms are almost always those that include utility work. For instance, once you start to renovate a kitchen, you will almost certainly find that you need plumbing and electrical work. It could include pulling out the built-in stove, wall oven, or sink with leaky sprayer; removing old linoleum from floor and walls; ripping out all the cabinets, the wall exhaust fan, and those old circular fluorescent light fixtures; or replacing everything, right down to the switches on the wall. All would be replaced with contemporary appliances, new flooring—probably of some modern, easily cleaned and wear-resistant material—and some recessed flood and task lighting. While you're at it, you would probably add a bay window or even a bump-out greenhouse/breakfast nook.

Renovation doesn't necessarily completely ignore the house's traditional history, but it is more intended to update the room or home and make it cater to the needs of the house's current occupants. Renovating even one room is an extensive undertaking and should be carefully planned to work around the best time of year for the project. You may not want to plan a major bathroom renovation just when the two college-age kids are going to be home for the summer!

ALERT!

Don't start tearing things apart until you investigate the safety of the materials. Hazardous materials, such as asbestos or lead paint, could be lurking in houses that were built in the era when these materials were in common use—before it was discovered that they cause respiratory problems, cancer, and other chronic and life-threatening conditions. Some materials require licensed professionals to do the destruction work.

Meeting Your Needs

Extensive renovation is often done to homes to accommodate an elderly occupant—such as creating nonskid surfaces or revamping bathrooms to make them safer. Or maybe you need to accommodate the needs of someone who is disabled by widening doorways and adding ramps to make the home wheelchair accessible.

A renovation may mean that instead of working on an existing room, you are actually adding a room to a home. Perhaps it's time to finally add that living room off the side of the house, the one you have dreamed of since you bought the place—where you could relax by a fire and watch the snow come down outside the floor-to-ceiling windows. Or maybe you've decided that now the kids are preteens, it's time to give them separate rooms, and a small two-story addition off the back of the house would solve that problem all at once. Adding a room is a common renovation project.

Remodeling Your Home

Renovation and remodeling are almost indistinguishable. Renovation is a major project that takes something that isn't working or is out of date—like plumbing and bathroom fixtures or the entire kitchen—and ripping it out and starting over. It's like getting a new house without starting from the ground up.

When you're remodeling, on the other hand, you may start a project like updating a kitchen, but instead of ripping everything out, you might replace the appliances, maybe change the red Formica countertops for blue, put down new linoleum, and perhaps even reface the existing cupboards. The difference here is that if you were going the renovation route, those cupboards would be torn out and replaced altogether, the appliance scheme would change, and the whole kitchen layout might even be different.

Remodeling, in other words, is more of an extensive "freshening up" but not as structural as a renovation. Remodeling and decorating can meet each other halfway; a minor remodel can amount to an extensive decoration. It depends on the focus of your project.

Planning Ahead

In order to determine the extent of what you want to do, it's critically important to plan your project and carefully assess what it is you are trying to accomplish. You really don't want a decorating project to turn into a remodeling project that you don't have the budget for. And you don't want to spend a few thousand dollars and weeks of time and frustration when you could have spent only a few hundred dollars, redecorated, and accomplished your overall goal for the room.

FACT

Did you decide that you enjoy decorating your own home so much and that you have such a knack for it you'd like to go into the business? Decorating Den Interiors has been around for over thirty years and offers independently owned franchises. Call ☎ 1-800-DEC-DENS.

How do you decide how far to go? That thing called planning rears its head again. Just exactly what do you need to accomplish? Look at a room from a goal perspective. If that dark little room off the second-floor bathroom is the only one you can spare for the sewing room you've always wanted, one main goal might be how to bring more light into the room. Do you want to remodel a little and add a window or skylight? Or will some decorating—in the form of removing dark wallpaper and painting the walls a light color as well as carefully planning the lighting scheme of the room—do the trick without the expense, mess, and time it would take to do the more extensive option?

Should You Make Extensive Changes?

Here are some things to keep in mind to help you decide the extent of your decorating project:

- *What is your budget for the room?* If you only have a budget of a few hundred dollars for that sewing room, you can assume that it won't foot the bill for a skylight. If your budget is a few thousand dollars, then a skylight can still be considered.
- *What is the priority status of the room?* Do you want to use the sewing room soon to make curtains and slipcovers for the rest of the house? If so, is it worth waiting to have a skylight installed before you can set up your sewing room? If you are busy moving into your new home and trying to settle into a new town, for instance, perhaps you

won't have time to use the sewing room for a few months anyway. In that case, maybe a skylight installation wouldn't interrupt you at all.

- *How often will you use the room?* If your sewing projects amount to simply sewing one or two things a year, do you really need to have your sewing machine set up in a separate room all the time? Perhaps redecorating another room to accommodate a sewing machine a couple times a year would do the trick. If you sew one project a month and like to sit down an hour at a time here and there without having to set everything up every time you want to sew, then a sewing room would take on a little more priority.

In order to make good decisions about your home, you need to really look closely and clearly at how you and your family use each room.

FACT

There are three Rs and a D of home improvements. *Restore*—to bring a home back to what it looked like when it was originally built. *Renovate*—to make major changes to improve or fix a home's functionality. *Remodel*—to make structural changes to create a new look for a room. *Decorate*—to create an atmosphere and mood in a room with color, furnishings, and accessories.

Decorating What You've Got

Now to the fun part! Decorating is what you are doing the minute you start to bring things into your new home or apartment and place them in rooms. Decorating your home is the most flexible and simplest of all the things you can do to your home—which means you can redecorate often. Some people redecorate for every season and every significant holiday, which means redecorating their homes several times a year.

Your Style

Your decorating style will change over the years as you gain more experience and live in different kinds of homes. Each time you will gain more insight, and as the years pass, the idea of redecorating several times a year probably won't seem daunting at all.

Even if you are moving into your first-ever home of your own, you probably are going to bring things with you that will form the basis of your decorating style. Maybe an original painting that you made payments on for two years at the local art gallery will be the focal point of your dining room. Perhaps for your college graduation, your parents gave you the massive sleigh bed that you had always coveted at the local furniture store. Or maybe your friends threw you a housewarming party with a fifties-themed gift requirement that began to shape the look of your kitchen.

Newlywed couples have the advantage of being able to register at their favorite stores and request specific home-related items that fit their decorating taste and not be at the mercy of well-meaning friends and family taking wild guesses.

Whatever the basis of your home furnishings, something will provide you with the impetus for decorating each room of your house. Sometimes that something isn't a thing at all. Often the room itself presents a certain style: tall ceilings, low ceilings, a patterned linoleum, built-in bookshelves, lots of windows, no windows—the possibilities are endless.

ESSENTIAL

Decorating should be fun. Don't get so serious or make it so complicated that decorating your house becomes overwhelming and exhausting. Less isn't always more with decorating, but make it your general plan to start with less and add more as you get a feel for the room you're decorating. Remember, the simpler your decoration job, the more things stand out.

Decorating can encompass any of the following:

- Changing the color scheme of a room through accessories, such as pillows, throw rugs, and other decorative elements.
- Changing the mood of a room by changing the decorative elements. An example might be softening a room by replacing wood furniture,

framed posters, and metal lamps with upholstered furniture, throw pillows, fabric art, and lamps with cloth shades.

- Completely redecorating a room, including buying new furniture, using different wall paint or paper, trim color, new rugs, drapes, or lighting, and changing, adding, or taking away knickknacks, wall art, and other decorative pieces.

How Often?

The fun part about decorating is that you can change your home's decoration as often as you like and on almost no budget at all. Shopping in flea markets and discount stores is a fun way to find unusual things (as described in Chapter 20). If your tastes are out of the mainstream, the discount shelves in the higher-end stores can often provide just the right things for you at significantly marked down prices.

Some rooms will beg to be redecorated more often than others. Think about the holidays—just putting a red and green tablecloth on the dining table creates a decorative theme for Christmas. By New Year's Day you will have probably tucked that holiday tablecloth away with the rest of the Christmas ornaments and decorations and replaced it with a more everyday one or a tablecloth with a snowflake pattern or something dark and wintery. That's redecorating at its simplest!

Do It Yourself?

If you can afford it, and you want to hire a decorator or designer who plans your decorating project and then implements the plan for you, that's great. But decorating is a perfect do-it-yourself activity. Hiring someone to do it all will mean missing out on a lot of fun. You can get the best of both worlds by hiring a decorating professional to help you plan a major redecoration and then implementing it yourself, getting tips from the pro on where to shop and the kinds of things to look for. Sometimes pros have an advantage in their ability to get into merchandise outlets that aren't open to the general public. Ⓔ

Chapter 2
Decorating Styles

You will want to pick a style for your home décor. And there are many to choose from! There are also many things to consider when picking that style—the most important one is, of course, your personal taste. However, another critical thing to consider when choosing how your house will be decorated is your lifestyle.

What's Your Lifestyle?

The Joneses have three active children ranging in age from six to fourteen. Both Sara and Sam Jones work full time in very demanding jobs. The family is constantly rushing around getting ready for school and work. On weekends, the kids often have friends visit to swim in the pool or play in the Jones's huge rec room. This family is not a candidate for decorating their home with white rugs and an extensive collection of glass figurines. They would just frustrate themselves and their kids, who really only want to act like young kids.

Jane and John Smith have several dogs and a small barn with a few horses. They both work at home as writers, so their house gets used twenty-four hours a day, seven days a week, with most meals eaten at home (meaning lots of dirty lots of dishes during the course of a day). They and the dogs track mud and dirt in the house. The Smiths' lifestyle isn't conducive to delicate decorations; they need sturdy carpeting, room in the kitchen for a dishwasher, and any features that make the house easy to clean.

Start your own personal decorating notebook now. Go through your pile of magazines and tear out the things that catch your eye. If you start to really accumulate clippings, organize them into categories (like "appliances") or by room. Then when you get serious about decorating a specific room, you can go to your notebook and pull out ideas for things you already know you like, and you have a good head start.

Elizabeth loves Victorian decorations. She always envisioned her house overflowing with wreaths and ribbons and chintz and brocade and heavy drapes and cherub statuettes. But Elizabeth absolutely hates to clean. Her salary as a paralegal does not allow her to add a house-cleaning service to her budget, especially since she pays a lot each month to rent her dream Victorian-style apartment. But dust is literally collecting on her decorating style. Elizabeth might try toning down her Victorian decorations either by eliminating half of them, relegating figurines and other hard-to-clean decorations to a couple of glass cabinets, or being true to the Victorian style in just one room that she can manage to dust and clean once every week or two.

Be honest about your lifestyle. Some key things to consider are these:

- *Do you like to entertain often?* Your decorating choices will need to reflect your desire to be constantly entertaining people. Maybe you should focus your efforts on the dining room if having dinner parties is what you do for fun.
- *Do you have children or plan to start a family soon?* It isn't fair to young children to decorate in a style that means you will constantly be reprimanding them. One way to help counteract that is to have room for a playroom where kids can be kids without any problem at all. And maybe you can designate one kid-free room where you can be true to your favorite decorating style and let the rest of the house be neutral ground for all.
- *Are pets a focal point of your life?* Dogs, cats, and even birds should be factored into your decorating choices. Keep things easy to clean, and avoid accumulating a lot of clutter for dog and cat hair to collect around. If you let pets get on the furniture, plan to use slipcovers or throw blankets that can be tossed in the washing machine on a regular basis.

There's a lot to think about when it comes to decorating your home before you even get around to selecting a specific style!

Architecture's Role

Does your home's basic architecture limit you in your choice of home decoration? The answer is, "It depends." What it really depends on is you. According to strict design and decorating protocol, it certainly isn't appropriate to decorate your Mission-style home in heavy Victorian furnishings. However, it is up to you and the other people who live in your home to decide how you want your home to look.

If you love Victoriana but you live in a Frank Lloyd Wright-inspired home in suburban Chicago, perhaps you could reserve one room for your Victorian tastes. You could scratch that Victorian itch by decorating your bedroom or your personal study in high Victorian style. In other words, if you choose a room that is private, who's going to care but you?

Many houses, especially those built in surburbia later in the twentieth century, are boxier and plainer, which may allow a lot more leeway in choosing what decorating style you might want. Square rooms with no architectural elements really do offer a blank canvas to work with.

Country Style

Country style is perhaps the easiest to grasp. The tendency is to be rustic, using decorative items that might be common in rural life. These items were often things that had a practical purpose around the farm and now either serve a new function or are just for decoration. Things like galvanized buckets or buckets formerly used for gathering maple syrup make great country-style cut flower containers. Furniture tends toward the comfortable and simple and is usually made of wood. If there is upholstery, the colors are deep and rich but not overly stylized. Fabrics—upholstery, table linens, and curtains—are usually made of cotton or wool.

ESSENTIAL

Fads come and go in quick order, so it's best to avoid fad-inspired decorating schemes. Trends, on the other hand, are contemporary styles that aren't as fleeting as fads. Trends, too, will change, but trendy styles tend to hang around long enough for you to be ready to redecorate anyway.

Primitive paintings of farm life make great country-style art choices as does most anything to do with animals. Fine nuances of style can come from exploring what country style is in many different countries—Italian country, French country, and American country often tend toward different color schemes such as floral or gingham check. Recently heart-shaped items have become a country-style staple, although whether you tend toward practical rustic or sweet rural is a matter of personal taste.

Country homes often have fireplaces and even firewood and the firewood holder are part of the country decorating scheme. Small farm tools can be buffed up and hung on walls, hung from ceilings, or stood in the corner as decorative elements. Pottery would go toward earthenware rather than porcelain, cut glass, or other more formal styles of glassware.

Country style doesn't have to be relegated to just those homes tucked at the edge of a field. This comforting decorating style can provide a warm homecoming when you close the door behind the city street of a metropolitan home.

Colonial Style

American colonial style is not so different from country style. You can think of this style as being typically more sparse and perhaps more practical. The colonists had what they brought with them, and while it included some of the more ornate furnishings in the Queen Anne and Chippendale styles, their homes also reflected everyday life with items that had everyday use, such as spinning wheels and quilting frames. Pewter was a material used for colonial dishware, and its use today gives a real taste of the era. Candle holders, both table and wall sconces, are classic colonial style. Rugs would be simple and probably still quite dark, with the brilliant colors we know today not as readily available to the common homeowner. Dining tables were plain and sturdy—cooking meals was an all-day affair, and eating was the social event of most days.

ALERT!

Don't get so caught up in trying to be true to a style that you blow your budget. Do what you can now, and remember that you can always add pieces later. Sometimes, after you live with a room for a while, you may change your mind about certain pieces you thought you wanted. You might decide not to add them after all and go with something different.

Traditional Style

The so-called traditional style of decorating is perhaps best defined by the word "elegance." Usually relating to a particular period in history, it is a decorating style that requires a true-to-the-period throughout-the-house approach. The traditional look is one of those things you know when you see it.

Window treatments are true drapes; not necessarily opulent, but full-length heavy fabric with formal tiebacks.

Think brass, Wedgwood china, Oriental rugs, and other classics. Furniture is upholstered wood, comfortable yet formal with stripes and floral patterns. In the type of house where this style is most appropriate, there are French doors, a formal dining room, wood floors to best show off the Oriental rugs, built-in bookcases and nooks for dishware displays, and a foyer.

Flower arrangements are formal and consist of traditional, old-fashioned flowers such as peonies and roses. The walls are dressed with hangings of formal paintings with semiornate frames and gilt-framed mirrors. Wall color is either white or light or dark reds and blues to show off formal decorations and furnishings.

Modern Style

The modern style is one of those revolving styles—what was "modern" in the 1970s falls into the "retro" category now!

Overall, however, "modern" typically refers to a decorating style that leans toward the sparse, with sharp edges and bold colors. The dining table may have a metal frame with a glass top and black metal chairs with fabric seats printed in a geometric pattern. White is usually the classic background color—white walls, for instance—that provide a plain backdrop for bold decorative items in red, black, deep blue, and other striking colors.

▲ A modern kitchen and dining table show a minimalist approach using crisp lines and shapes.

For artwork, you might lean toward posters or reproductions of abstract masters such as Miró or Picasso. Minimal is the key word—floral bouquets make great modern decorative elements, but skip the country wildflowers in the old "chamberpot." Modern style requires a huge bold bouquet of brilliantly colored flowers, probably just one or two kinds of the same or similar color—think bright against a stark background of white and black surroundings.

FACT

Style-specific magazines make great resources for ideas and inspiration. *Traditional Home, Coastal Living, Country Living,* and *Natural Home* are just a small selection of magazines on the newsstand that you can pick from to help create your chosen home décor. See Appendix A for a longer list.

Modern style also yearns for the unique. Oddly shaped chairs, spiral staircases, and found objects placed in a surprising way are great ways to express your modern instincts.

Victorian Style

Ornate, flowery, and heavy styling in gilt, brass, and chenille are the key concepts for the Victorian era. Deciding to decorate in Victorian gives you the go-ahead to be opulent, flamboyant, and excessive!

The 1800s Victorian era gave us the bathroom, and if you want to do just one room in your house in this style, the bathroom is it. Choose heavy curtains layered with off-white lace, an ornate pedestal sink, and clawfoot tub. If you have the space, one or two pieces of dark furniture— such as a small accessories table and a heavily upholstered, uniquely shaped chair—make perfect Victorian bathroom furnishings. Add some brass fixtures, marbleize the walls, and you have the style.

The rest of the house is equally ornate when properly decorated in the Victorian style. If you hate to dust and vacuum, and you don't have a housekeeper, forget it! But if you still insist on decorating in this style, then start shopping for friezes and border trims for the walls, shop the antique and secondhand stores for floral paintings with heavy frames, and throw pillows, pillows, and more pillows, some with fringe, on your dark upholstered furniture.

FACT

For information on everything Victorian, join the Victorian Society of America at: 219 South Sixth Street, Philadelphia, PA 19106; ✆ (215) 627-4252; on the Web at ✑ *www.victoriansociety.org*). The Victorian Society is self-described as "dedicated to the protection, understanding, education, and enjoyment of your nineteenth-century heritage."

Despite its overly ornate styling, the "clutter" of Victorian décor can feel very cozy and casual. If you have large rooms in an expansive house, you will have to work hard to really accomplish this style throughout the house! Plan to find at least one oversized piece or full suite of furniture to dominate the space in large rooms, and then work around it.

Arts & Crafts Style

The Arts & Crafts movement started in England. Perhaps one of the best-known craftsmen of this style is William Morris. In the mid-1800s, amidst the ornate Victorian era, Morris brought fine attention to detail and craftsmanship in the carpets, beautiful wallpapers, furnishings, and accessory designs that his company produced. The American Arts & Crafts style took off when the mundane repetitiveness of industrialization and its resulting mass-made materials gave way to the desire for real art.

But one of Morris's frustrations, which other members of the early movement shared, was the fact that all of the attention to detail and individual craftsmanship also put the costs out of reach for many people. At some point, artisanship and mass production combined, turning the Arts & Crafts style into something that could be had by more than just the wealthy who could afford the handmade wallpapers, fabrics, and furniture.

The term "Arts & Crafts" is used interchangeably with "Craftsman style," which is a term the famous furniture maker Gustav Stickley gave to his handcrafted furnishings. You will also hear the term "Mission" used to describe this period, a term that came from the simple furnishings of actual mission houses.

There are many outlets for Arts & Crafts style furnishings where you can shop to create your home's look. If your budget is large, you can shop for antiques from the period itself. If your budget is medium to large, you can find many quality reproductions of Stickley furniture and Morris wallpapers. Even the less expensive home furnishings outlets and department stores are offering pieces in the Arts & Crafts style. Some of these lack the solid feel of the original intent, but they can offer the look. If you are handy, you can also find many Craftsman-style furniture kits and plans.

Although a room decorated in the Arts & Crafts style can be highly ornate, it is more each individual piece than the overall effect that is heavily decorated. A room may therefore look somewhat sparse in furnishings, but what is there is highly styled.

Retro Style

Retro style often refers to the 1950s era—think high-chrome diner décor, linoleum with strong geometric patterns, and lots of strong color like Fiestaware china and a bright red canister set with matching breadbox. But retro style these days mostly just means hearkening back to a specific era in the twentieth century, not just the 1950s.

Shopping for retro decorating accessories can be lots of fun. The perfect item will be hiding in the back corner of that "antiques and junque" shop you've passed by a million times.

You can decorate in the hippie style of the 1960s with fabric in baby blue and large yellow flowers, lava lamps, Naugahyde recliners, shag carpets—now creeping back into mainstream fashion anyway—and televisions with lots of wood. Old decorating books from used bookstores and vintage shows on Nickelodeon will help you get these retro styles down perfectly.

And you don't even have to despair about the kitchen—modern appliances in retro styling are available if you are so married to the style that you are willing to spend the extra money for these highly stylized appliances.

Cottage Style

Cottage style can refer to either seaside cottage or country cottage.

Decorating in a coastal style would mean using elements reminiscent of water and sky as well as the following:

- White-painted walls, often with beaded wainscoting
- White wicker furniture and reed carpets
- Trim, furniture, or ceilings painted light blue
- Breezy curtains of lightweight and light-colored cotton
- Accessories like beach rocks and shells

Instead of the light, airy, breezy effect found in coastal cottage style, country cottage style aims for a cozier, darker effect, and decorations would go toward the more heavy natural elements like the following.

- Rustic, stick-style furniture
- Dark wood dressers
- Buckets full of dark country flowers
- A heavy oak table
- Dark red or blue or gingham-check curtains
- Woven wool rugs

Cottage style is usually somewhat quaint but more comfortable than cute. Typically, a cottage would be small, and the furnishings would be comfy but few, and most everything is practical. For instance, chairs may be of a type that can also be used outside, since lives lived in cottages usually included a lot of outdoor time.

Southwest Style

Southwestern style is one of the decorating styles that is very much tied to a region and its natural surroundings. Think pottery accessories, sand and sunset colors, cactus plants, and dark weavings accented with bright colors.

QUESTION?

What does "eclectic" mean?
In terms of style, the dictionary definition of "eclectic" is "selecting what appears to be best in various doctrines, methods, or styles" with a secondary definition of "components of elements drawn from various sources." When it comes to decorating, if someone refers to your decorating style as eclectic, it means that you have mixed several styles into your decorating scheme, perhaps a different style in different rooms or even more than one style in the same room. There are no set rules; do what's right for you. It's okay to be eclectic!

Although Southwestern style comes from the southwest region of the United States, you certainly don't have to live in New Mexico or Arizona to decorate in this popular style. You will find Southwestern décor in any part of the country. Shopping online and through catalogs—and taking advantage of the increasing popularity of home stores—makes it simple to order almost anything Southwestern, even if you live in northern Maine.

Follow Your Instincts

These nine modes we've reviewed represent just some of the basic decorating styles. There are many more, as well as some tailored versions of each of these.

If you aren't really sure what style you like, narrow your choices down to two or three. Study books and magazines that showcase those styles, and visit some showrooms at furniture stores. Larger furniture stores—there are some you can get lost in!—tend to have entire rooms furnished in one style so you can actually sit in a chair and feel the style all around you. Take advantage of their extensive collections and the expertise of their staff in helping you understand your own decorating preferences and in finding just the things you are looking for to complete the look of your home.

Chapter 3

Where to Begin

Whether you are tackling a whole house or doing a decorating makeover on just one room, planning is the place to begin. If you plan well and do all your shopping ahead of time so that everything you need is at your fingertips, you can probably finish a significant redecorating job on one room over a long weekend.

Major Considerations

Sometimes decorating isn't a huge overall project. Decorating your home also includes impulse purchases and small objects that you are looking for to fill in a gap, like a picture for a blank wall space, just the right vase or lamp for the endtable, or something new to spruce up the mantle. These kinds of things don't take the overall planning that major projects do, but they should be carefully purchased to fit in with your decorating scheme. In later chapters, we will get into the accessories and flea market purchases and even some projects to make yourself. In the meantime, there are some big things to cover.

Before you begin to do things like move a single item in or out of your house, choose new paint for your walls or trim, or whatever your redecorating scheme entails, you need to think about the three main considerations in planning a home decorating project:

- How much money do you have to devote to the project?
- How much time do you have allotted to do the job?
- What special tools or items will you need?

Budget

Is "not much" the operative phrase for your decorating budget? That's no reason to despair; decorating on a tight budget can be the most fun of all! However, if your budget is small, plan (there's that word again!) for extra time to finish your decorating job. You will want to do lots of shopping around in out-of-the-way places and perhaps make some things yourself—curtains, table linens, a lamp shade—so you will need the time to do that. If your finances for the project are more extensive, that's great, but it is always good to budget even if the budget is well padded.

How *do* you budget for decorating? That may be as simple as the plain fact that you have, say, $600 to redecorate the dining room. This amount pretty much rules out a new dining room table from being part of the plan. But if you really just want to brighten up the room, a $600 budget can buy some perfect table linens, a couple of colorful pitchers to use as flower vases, a new mirror, and some other accessories. Voilà!

Your dining room has a fresh new look.

If your decorating ideas go beyond linens and pottery, you will want to consider every element of the room and do some price shopping so you can be realistic about the amount you should budget. The chapters later in this book on specific rooms include sample budget charts specific to those rooms.

If you are planning a major redecoration of your entire home or you are just moving into a new home and are starting your decorating from scratch, you may even want to go so far as to take out a home improvement loan. If borrowing money is part of your potential plan, this is a good reason to develop a detailed plan of each room and take some time to get a real sense of what you want to do.

Time

Time and *timing* are important. How much time do you have to put into the decorating job? This can guide you in your major decisions. Is it something you can do in small bits of time over the course of a couple of months? If so, you may want to design your redecoration in individual segments that you can complete and move on to the next segment when you are ready. Or is the job something you want to get done all at once? Perhaps you have a deadline in the form of an event or special dinner party you are hosting. If you simply have to get it done by next weekend, that may mean you need to shop in places that are close by. You will not be able to catch the big sale at the huge furniture store a hundred miles away.

Many people wait until they are preparing their home to sell before they get into fixing it up the way they always wanted to. Don't wait until you aren't going to be living in your house any longer—decorate now and enjoy it!

When is a good time to do the decorating project? Don't forget timing your project appropriately. You don't want to be redecorating the family room just when a bunch of friends are coming over for your big Super Bowl party. Maybe redecorating the family room is a good thing to do in the fall, when the kids have just gone back to school and the weather is still warm enough for them to spend most afternoons outside. If you have only one bathroom, a redecorating project for that room may be best left for when your spouse is out of town—at the very least, don't start it the weekend before you are having visitors come for an extended stay! Visualize what is going to have to take place for your decorating job to happen, and plan accordingly.

Tools

What kinds of things do you need to get the job done? If you will be painting the walls, don't get so absorbed in picking the color that you forget to stock up on the right brushes, rollers, edgers, paint can openers, drop cloths, and so on. Wallpapering is another task that requires specific supplies. Are you hanging new curtains? Will they fit on the old rods, or do you need to buy new ones?

If you are moving furniture around, you will want some shims to be sure the cabinet is level in its new spot, for example. If you are stripping the room to bare walls and putting up new art and mirrors, buy a picture-hanging kit. These inexpensive kits typically come in plastic compartmentalized containers, offering a wide selection of sizes with nails of the appropriate size as well as hanging wire and screws. Having this kind of thing on hand means you won't be tempted to pound a rusty old nail in the wall just to get your picture hung.

ALERT!

The rise-and-run proportions of stairs are designed according to standard measurements to meet safety standards. But if you are planning to buy carpeting, stencils, or runners for your stairs, always measure them anyway despite the supposed standards, especially in older houses that were built before safety standards were created and where stairs were just stuck in wherever there was a well of space to accommodate them.

Although it is almost inevitable that you will realize partway through your project that you are missing something you need that requires another trip to the store, you can keep this to a minimum by planning and visualizing your project in advance.

Don't Overwhelm Yourself

Decorating should be fun. Don't make it stressful by forcing yourself into a major project that you hadn't intended on coping with. Maybe all the living room needs is new slipcovers for the upholstered furniture, some throw pillows, and a little rearranging; do this, and you've solved your need to freshen it up. Don't wait until you've pulled out all the heavy furniture, disconnected the complex electronic equipment, and torn the wallpaper off the walls to decide that you really never wanted to get in so deep. Think it through before you touch a thing, and by all means talk it through with the other family members.

Important Questions

Here are some questions to ask yourself before you begin a decorating project:

- What am I trying to accomplish?
- What works about this room?
- What doesn't work about this room?
- What kind of activities does this room play host to?
- Who uses this room the most?
- Is there another use for this room that I want to encourage?
- What kind of atmosphere do I want this room to have?

The answers to these questions will help you start to decide what to concentrate on and what to leave alone in the room. If your bedroom is really used only for sleeping, then your choices of decoration will probably be quite different from those you'd make if you retreated to the room with a good book every morning for a couple of hours. Accommodations for sleeping require only a comfortable bed and a mood conducive to restfulness. Reading involves considerations like lighting requirements, a good chair or bed that allows you to prop yourself up with a book, and a nightstand or side table for a cup of coffee and where you can leave your book behind until next time.

Planning

Start the planning process with a paper and pencil. List in general the things you will want to buy, like lamps, lampshades, wall art, new switchplates, paint for the dresser, or a new throw rug.

Once you know what your overall needs are, begin to refine them. Go through the questions listed above so you can begin to decide specifics: "sage-green paint for the old dresser with mirror" or "matching pierced lampshades for the wall lamp and the table lamp."

Color will likely dictate everything; it's so important you'll find an entire chapter on color in this book.

There are several computer programs available to give you some assistance with a redecorating project. Many come specific to a room in the house—kitchen and bathroom especially—and even outdoor landscaping design. These programs can help with things like color choices and furniture placement.

Your overall decisions about what kind of mood you want the room to have will influence almost every other decision you make for the room. This is particularly true of your color choices. If you want a quiet, peaceful room and therefore decide to paint the walls sage green, then off-white lampshades might better be in keeping with the more subdued mood than stark white ones. Say you removed a white plaster ceiling and exposed the beams in your post-and-beam farmhouse dining room. When the ceiling was white, the dark red wallpaper seemed fine, but now the ceiling is darker, it seems more appropriate for the walls to be lighter. Color, or lack of it, is everything in home decorating.

Taking Measurements

A good place to start in any room is to take measurements to have on hand when you shop. To be a frugal shopper, you need to hit the sales, be willing to stop at out-of-the-way stores on your way home from a business trip to the city, and simply be ready to buy on impulse. You don't want to leave behind that perfect throw rug for the foyer that is half price in a going-out-of-business sale just because you have no idea if it would fit or not. And to drive back to an out-of-the-way store could cost more in time and money than the savings amount—not to mention the risk that the rug could be gone.

▲ Some large furniture—like a baby grand piano—will necessarily be a focal point of the room it is in. Use this to your advantage and work to emphasize the piece. Here, the piano is given a spot in a prime location in this alcove surrounded by windows.

Your best bet is to have the measurements on hand, so you can immediately know for certain whether the piece of furniture you've just fallen in love with will fit in the space you have.

The Area of the Entire Room

Measure the dimensions of the room. If you are planning wall-to-wall carpeting, fractions of an inch are important (and the installers will measure for you). But rounding off in whole inches is fine for things like planning the size of chairs and sofas and area rugs. Mark off any spaces that are used by things like radiators and built-in bookcases so you can be sure to accommodate them when choosing furniture and rugs.

Parts of the Room

If the rooms in your house have little alcoves and odd areas that might make isolated spaces for a specific piece of furniture, take the measurement of these. You don't want to choose the perfect oversized chair for a cozy nook that you plan to read in, only to find that it is a tad *too* oversized and leaves no room for anything else, like a small side table where you can put a cup of tea or a reading lamp.

Odd Wall Spaces

Do you want to hang a painting over the living room fireplace mantel? Measure the width of the mantel and the height from the mantel to the ceiling. You may assume you want the painting to only be a portion of that size, but take the overall measurement anyway just in case you see something perfect that is a bit larger than what you were originally thinking of getting. Have on hand other wall measurements as well, like the space between the two windows on the side wall or the area between the doorway and the kitchen pass-through. Also measure things like the distance from the floor to the bottom edge of windows in case you later decide to place something—like a work table or small bookcase—at the window.

Windows

Measuring windows for curtains and drapes can be tricky. If you know exactly what kind of window treatments you plan to use or you are replacing existing drapes and will use the rods that are already in place, then you may already know which measurement to use. But if you aren't sure, you need to know the measurements from both the inside of the casing and the outside edge of the window trim. Most simple curtains can be easily shortened if they are too long, but be careful of that if the curtains have ruffles or fluted edges on the bottom—these are not easily shortened and you will want to be certain to buy the right length.

Odd Measurements

Although you are not likely to be placing furniture in doorways, you do need to get pieces *through* doorways. Measure all doorways in the house so you can know for sure that you can actually get a piece in the house to the room you bought it for.

ALERT!

Depending on your project, there may be other measurements you'll need. Measurements like dimensions of cabinet shelves for shelf paper and those kinds of smaller specifics will be covered in the chapters on specific rooms, so be sure to read the chapter related to the room you are working on before you begin.

Hiring Professionals

Chances are good that at some point in your lifetime, you will hire a professional or two to help with your decorating projects. It's fun and usually less expensive to do things yourself, but there are some things that are more easily left to those with lots of experience. Painters, wallpaper hangers, and carpet installers all have enough experience to know the tricks of the trade that allow them to make the finished job look professional. If you watch them as they go, you may be surprised to see that they make some of the same little inevitable mistakes and

THE EVERYTHING HOME DECORATING BOOK

messes that you might have made, but you will also notice that they know how to hide them and fix them so that the final job is clean, neat, and polished.

Your budget may not be large enough to include much outside help. But if there is a significant element of your redecorating plan that is beyond your expertise and is key to the whole look, you might consider squeezing enough into your budget for a pro.

Finding the Right Person

Everyone has heard, of course, disaster stories about so-called professionals who take your money and do a less-than-professional job. But there are lots of things you can do to lower your chances of getting ripped off.

First and foremost, ask for recommendations from friends, neighbors, friends of friends, your hairdresser, and especially other professionals you have worked with and respect. You may think your electrician wouldn't know anything about wallpapering, but perhaps he has done electrical work for several clients who have all used the same wallpapering pro. By making just a couple of calls to them, you can find that they all use the same guy because he is good and his price is fair. The same goes for any professional contractor you need—you can usually trust other contractors to be a good judge, since they are putting their own reputations on the line by recommending someone else.

ALERT!

Unless you are using a professional you have worked with before, always get three quotes from three different pros for any job that is more significant than a few hundred dollars. With three estimates to compare, you can not only see price differences but you can also get a sense of who you have the best rapport with and who gets back to you in a timely fashion (which may have some bearing on how timely they will be in completing their jobs). Two other things should factor into your decision: recommendations from people you trust who have used the pro, and—if possible—a personal visit to some of the pro's finished projects.

Know what you want done, and don't let the contractor talk you into several other things. That's a great way to blow your budget. If you want to paint the hall yourself but have someone do the wallpaper in the formal living room, paint the hall yourself. And be careful of a lot of "add-ons." Some may be helpful to your overall plan, but many are just putting more money in the pocket of the contractor.

Here are some great things to leave to the professional contractors:

- Sanding and refinishing wood floors (of any type of wood)
- Complex wallpapering jobs with expensive wallpaper in complex patterns
- Significant plaster repair that needs to be done before you paint
- Hanging doors
- Installing linoleum and wall-to-wall carpeting (and removing the old)

Be Prepared!

Having contractors in the house is disruptive, plain and simple. Be prepared to have to move out of a room. If you are having professionals come in and work in the bathroom, be sure you have alternative facilities. If your kitchen is going to be a mess for a week, be sure to have ready-made meals in the fridge, and move the microwave oven into another room where it is accessible and not covered in dust and dropcloths.

With good planning and understanding of the process, hiring a professional to do some of your decorating work can mean money well spent. The finished job will be a pleasure to look at and fun to finish decorating.

Hiring a Decorating Consultant

Decorating consultants are a great help when it comes to formulating the decorating style of your home. If you are starting from scratch with a large house, you do a lot of entertaining, and you don't have a great knack for decorating, a decorating professional will be just the thing to make sure the ways that you choose to decorate your home suit your tastes and your lifestyle.

Decorating professionals can also serve a great purpose in helping a couple come to common ground on decorating projects at which they are at odds. The pros know how to account for the tastes and needs of both sides—even when they are seemingly completely opposite—and come up with solutions that can satisfy both parties.

The professional decorator also has all the leads on the supply houses and great decorating stores where the best wallpaper can be found for the best price and where to look for some unique selections.

They are knowledgeable about color and fabrics and textures and materials, and they can lead you in the right direction. And if you still want to do some of it yourself, you can talk with the decorator to come up with what he or she will do and when you will take over. You can also set a consulting rate, so if you get stuck after the decorator has completed his or her part, you can get still a consult with the decorator as you're working.

Chapter 4
Color

Using color in your home is both an art and a science. A room can be made to look larger, smaller, more cheerful, or cozier with just a can of paint. If a room with dark walls appears dreary, a few splashes of bright color from throw pillows, artwork, or other simple accessories can turn the room around. Color is key when you make home decorating decisions.

Experimenting with Color

You will want to use color with discretion, but don't be afraid to use bold colors when decorating your home. If the color you choose for the walls turns out to be a little too bold, there's always more paint at the paint store—but before you start repainting to tone the color down, live with it a week or so. Put up some wall accessories and move some furniture into place. You may find that the color begins to take on the form of an enhancement that makes other things stand out nicely rather than being the overriding element in the room.

◀ Don't forget that the floor is another spot to add color to a room. Colorful tiles and a toilet seat help blend the colors of the floor with the lighter colored walls.

The color wheel can help you experiment with more chance of success. The basic color wheel consists of the three primary colors: red, blue, and yellow. A more complex color wheel includes the secondary colors—green, orange, and purple—each of which is made by combining two of the three primary colors. The twelve-part color wheel is the most useful wheel when it comes to decorating. It includes the tertiary colors, which are made by shading the secondaries with a primary hue (green-yellow, for instance, or orange-red). These shades are known as "analogous." Each secondary color has a primary "complement" that it cannot combine with to form a new shade. The complement is the primary color that was not used to form the secondary. Purple's complement is yellow; we have tertiary shades of purple-blue and purple-red, but there is no shade called purple-yellow.

FACT

Some of the most common decorating mistakes can be avoided by good use of color. Color can correct a room that is off-balance. It can give a room a cohesive look. It can compensate for a decorating scheme that ignores the room's focal point, and it can make it less obtrusive if lighting is used incorrectly.

Analogous colors are side by side on the twelve-part color wheel. Complementary colors are opposite each other on the twelve-part color wheel. What a color does in and to a room depends entirely on its relation to other colors in the room. Use the color wheel to help guide you before you make any significant decisions about color combinations.

Using Color Effectively

Always consider breaking "the rules" when it comes to home decorating. However, you can't break the rules unless you know what they are. Here are some basic guidelines to follow using color:

- Don't overdo the number of colors you use in one room. Keep the number to between two and four, depending on the size of the room.
- Decide whether you are going to emphasize the furnishings or the background.
- Coordinate the color of a room with the color of an adjoining room or rooms if you can see one from the other.
- Use neutral colors to camouflage defects, such as architectural or structural problems, that you can't easily change. Use bold colors to enhance interesting architectural details.
- Use patterns to make a neutral background more interesting.
- You can get away with more than one pattern in a room if the patterns use the same color scheme.

You can read everything on color matching and what impact color has on mood, balance, focus, and so on, but when all is said and done, you need to like the colors you use in your home. Don't feel compelled to use colors you don't like just for the sake of using color. If blue makes you feel depressed, give it a pass. If yellow gives you a headache, don't paint walls in your house this color and buy extra ibuprofen to compensate. Just find another color.

How a color really looks depends a lot on what kind of light it will be seen under. Fluorescent lighting makes most colors look stark and somewhat bold. Incandescent light casts a warm glow on most color, but only in small splashes, leaving parts of the wall looking warm and cheerful and other parts darker. Natural light is, of course, the best lighting of all for showing the true color of a room. But even with great natural light, a color will always need to stand up to your home's lighting when it is dark outside.

The Color on Your Walls

Like with everything else in home decorating, choosing a color requires some planning. You probably already have some favorite colors that you certainly should feel free to incorporate into your home decorating scheme. No one spends more time in your house than you, so enjoy it with the colors you love!

Since the walls usually show the largest expanse of color in any room, let's start there. Decide what the overriding use of the room is. Knowing that the room is used for relaxing, that it is intended to be a stimulating environment for a child, or that it is a creative, inspiring place for an artist will have a huge impact on your decision concerning the best colors for the room.

Next, consider whether the room has a focal point. This might be one you put there, such as a painting or a standout piece of furniture on the scale of a baby grand piano. Your focal point might also be built-in, like a fireplace or a dramatic bank of window perhaps with an equally dramatic view. That focal piece should be considered when you're choosing color. Don't make the rest of the room so compelling that this centerpiece no longer stands out; few rooms are large enough to accommodate two focal points!

FACT

If a room in your home seems small, you don't have to get out the sledgehammer. It is much easier to make the room appear larger by using color to create the illusion of greater size. Instead of removing walls (which is often impossible anyway), paint them white or a light color to make the room seem more spacious. A classic rule of thumb is that light colors make rooms seem larger, while dark colors make rooms seem smaller.

You'll also need to take into account the size of the room. If the room is large, do you want to make it seem smaller? Or vice versa with a small room? Sometimes rooms are okay the size they are, so don't think just because a room is small it needs to look larger. Painting the trim the same color as the walls will help make a small room seem larger. Contrasting color trim will make the elements of the room stand out more. This makes them more noticeable, and the more noticeable the elements of a room, the more they can seem to take up space. Making a room feel smaller isn't as odd as it might sound at first. It may be that you want a room to seem cozier than it is. A darker color for the walls is the way to start. From there, you can use tricks of furniture arrangement and lighting to make reading nooks, conversation areas, or an intimate dining space break a large room up into smaller pieces.

Can you see other rooms of the house from this room? What will the effect of a certain color in one room have on those other rooms that are also visible? You don't want the house to look like a rainbow as you look from one room into others—or perhaps you do. That's the thing with home decorating, almost anything goes!

Beyond the Walls

You might begin your color planning with the walls of a room. As we've already mentioned, if the room accommodates a strong architectural element or if the room will hold a strong piece of furniture like a canopy bed or heirloom dining set, you will want to take that into consideration first and then think about the walls.

But small things can have a great impact, too, when they are either bold in color or boldly inserted into certain color schemes. Perhaps you painted the dining room walls and the woodwork white, and in that built-in set of shelves you set a fairly large collection of deep red glassware against the bright white. Red is a color that is bold and dramatic. Sprinkle some red in the rest of the room—such as red blossoms in floral arrangements, red accents in an otherwise neutral painting, or a red Persian carpet. Suddenly, even though the walls are neutral, people will start referring to it as "the red room." Color has impact!

◀ Contrast light colored walls with furniture in bold, deep colors or patterns.

You can do the opposite with boldly painted walls. If a room's walls are deep blue, significant white accents—white trim, a white statuette, white linens, even a white rug—can switch the focus of the whole room from the blue walls to the white accessories.

Speaking of rugs, you don't want to forget the floor when it comes to color. If the floors in your home are wood and are in great shape, you probably won't want to paint them. However, if the wood is less than lovely or is flawed, painting them can be a nice way to keep wood floors while covering up the flaws.

If you are trying to create a color scheme, take samples along whenever possible. Perhaps you've chosen a wallpaper for your dining room and are now looking for upholstery for the chair seats and rugs. Clip off a patch of the wallpaper large enough to show all the colors in the paper and keep it by your side as you shop.

Cottages almost beg for painted wood floors—white, light gray, and light blue are common colors for making a summer home feel cool and fresh. You can also paint wood floors rather dramatically—if the expanse appears too over-the-top in bright red, cover a lot of the floor with scatter rugs. Once you get the furniture and rugs in place, the red—or blue or green—will come through around the edges as an accent.

Forget Color Stereotypes

You don't want to pigeonhole colors into a certain style. Black-and-white floors can be country casual or metropolitan high style. Brilliant green can be a bold streak in a retro diner style or the backdrop to a collection of Old World cooking utensils. What a color does depends on how, where, and with what you use it. If you like a color but don't think of it as right for the style of your home, use it and work with other things to make it right!

Colors don't have to be bold and contrasting to make a strong decorating statement. Consider many tones of neutral in a room, and use textures like heavily woven fabrics on cushions or fabrics like brocade that offer depth while barely changing in color at all. You can then add a couple of splashes of strong color if you want, or you can incorporate more dramatic neutral pieces like plants or unique furniture.

Visualizing Colors That Work

If you are concerned about simply trying a color out, you can attempt to see it in action before you see it in your own home. Start by looking in all the picture books and home magazines that you can get your hands on. Don't get too hung up on home style, and instead just look for color combinations. Notice what draws your eye; that might help you choose colors.

Finding Examples

A good source for photos is the Internet, which is host to hundreds of home decorating Web sites complete with pictures. Again, look for color combinations that intrigue you.

Visit large home furnishings stores—IKEA, Pier 1 Imports, Ethan Allen, as well as local merchants—where several vignettes for each room are set up to allow shoppers to visualize the furnishings in a finished setting. A lot of these places also have Web sites.

Making Examples

If you have a certain unusual combination in mind, you may not be able to find an example in photos. One way you can get an idea of how they work together is to look for fabrics in those colors and hold them together. If you can afford to really experiment, buy a yard or two of fabrics in the colors you are considering. Drape them in the room. Cut tiny swatches and accent larger pieces with those, or set pieces of colored dishware and pottery on the fabric to get a look at certain colors together. With the range of bed linens available today, you could do this with bed sheets as well—and if you don't cut them, you'll also have useable sheets!

You might also want to paint a piece of plywood or board and use it to experiment in a room. If that still doesn't do it for you, go ahead and find a small space in the room that you can paint—not just a patch across one expanse of wall, but a spot that is somewhat contained where you could really envision the color. Hold up some fabrics, place a picture or a pot, and get a real sense of what the color will look like on the wall.

If you do this, prepare the wall first. Remove any wallpaper, or sand the old paint surface and paint a coat of primer on. Then be prepared to paint at least two coats of the paint color, maybe three depending on the under-surface. If you can, choose a place near some trim and paint that too. Then you can really get see the colors in action. If you are really taking a risk with color, this can all be well worth your while. This is especially true if the room you are painting is large and it would mean spending a lot of time and money on quality paint just to find out that once you got the color on the wall, you simply couldn't live with it.

FACT

There are lots of great Web sites devoted to color. Check out any of the paint manufacturers' sites for color tips and ideas, such as Benjamin Moore (✍ *www.benjaminmoore.com*). Another color site is ✍ *www.colormatters.com*, where you can learn all sorts of bits of information about color to help you choose colors and hues in your home and where you can also learn about color theory and color and design.

Achieving Different Styles with Color

Some decorating styles can almost be accomplished simply by using certain colors and color combinations. Some styles just wouldn't use some colors. For example, here are some color specifics about some of the significant decorating styles:

- In the post-Colonial 1700s, lighter colors became more fashionable. In Colonial decorating, darker earthy colors brought about by the materials of the day—wood and pewter, for instance—would be used.
- Even in the Victorian era, which made its mark using deep rich colors in unusual combinations, lighter colors were common in the kitchen.
- The Art Deco style used pale colors with deep strong accent colors.
- The 1950s and the onslaught of mass-produced items for the home

brought us some exciting colors that were used—and perhaps a bit overused.

• Southwestern style is evoked with earth tones of browns and terra cotta mixed with splashes of brilliant yellow, light blue, pink, and white.

White enhances any bold color, making it even bolder than it is by itself. White can also soften colors, or it can serve to blend colors that aren't necessarily good side by side. Don't pick bold colors and just let them run together. Instead, offset them with white walls or white furnishings, and let them come alive.

Use your imagination, and be creative in thinking about the colors of a room. Take lessons from nature in mixing colors. Look at artwork to see what combinations attract your eye. No matter what you learn about color, the key to making your home attractive is that you and your family need to like what you see. Above all, therefore, make sure your own tastes dictate your choice of colors in your home.

QUESTION?

How can color affect the size of a room?
If you want to make a room appear to have higher ceilings, be sure the ceiling is painted in a light color compared to the walls. Make a larger room more intimate by painting the walls in a dark color. Conversely, make a smaller room appear larger with light-colored walls. Stick to shades like blue and white to give a room a cool, light, breezy air and to make it feel bigger than it is.

Chapter 5
Feng Shui

The ancient Chinese concept called *feng shui* (pronounced "fung shway," with *feng* meaning "wind" and *shui* meaning "water") has been increasingly infiltrating the American home design and decorating scene over the past ten or twenty years. Feng shui teaches that through the careful use and positioning of different basic elements, you can create a positive influence on your life. This chapter will help you get started today!

What Is Feng Shui?

Practicing feng shui doesn't mean you have to fill your house with bamboo flutes, crystals, wind chimes, or other decorative items you may not even like. Feng shui is a way of being, not just furniture placement or a way of creating greater wealth.

We all know how it is when a room just feels right. We know when our lives are going along smoothly and even the bumps in the road are not devastating, when our homes add to our well being, and when we simply feel comfortable. Feng shui is just another way to say we have influence over that feeling of well being in our own homes.

History

Feng shui as a concept has been around for thousands of years. The earliest references to it have been discovered in texts dating back to 200 B.C., although perhaps not always under the same name. The result of good feng shui in an environment is good health, prosperity, and good luck.

Some of the fundamentals of feng shui seem like simple common sense. Positioning a house to take advantage of southern sun in cold winters and using the natural environment like mountains and trees to protect a home from cold winds are principles of good site design that have been in practice since ancient Chinese civilization began. But feng shui goes deeper than those surface considerations. It encompasses cosmic influences like those expressed in the *I Ching* (the pre-Taoist text also known as *The Book of Changes*). In practice, feng shui can produce the mystical sense one gets from watching a dowsing rod point to a water source.

The Basic Premise

The basic premise of feng shui evolved from the simple idea that people are affected—either negatively or positively—by their surroundings, including the layout and orientation of their homes and workspaces. The goal of practicing feng shui is to take advantage of the positive influences of your surroundings in their relation to the primary energy movers in the environment (that is, wind and water). You can do this by moving, replacing, and redirecting things to help in that pursuit.

To achieve balance through feng shui principles, there are many things to consider. Compass direction, materials, and color are among the key things that the dictates of feng shui require you to take into consideration if you use the concept to help decorate your home.

Like the Chinese practice of acupuncture that balances the energy flow in the body, feng shui balances the energy flow of an environment, which in this case would be your home. In the body, the energy manipulated by acupuncture flows along various body channels called "meridians." The meridians in your home are hallways and doorways—elements that are part of the structure of the house—as well as the pathways that you create depending on how you place your furnishings. The result of good feng shui is a harmonious environment where energy (or ch'i) moves with ease. The goal is to keep energy from getting blocked or bottled up in any one area and from letting it get swept along without advantage.

Controlling Energy

Energy and its flow are of supreme importance in the Chinese approach to health and harmony. The free flow of energy through a house can mean the difference between health or sickness, wealth or financial problems, and harmonious relationships or constant arguments.

Perhaps the most common problem is energy getting blocked or bottled up in certain places in the home. Energy is dynamic, constantly moving and changing, never static yet cyclical in nature. But it is also possible for energy to flow too freely and be lost before you have the chance to use it to your advantage. Feng shui practice has cures for this energy illness as well.

Blocked Energy

Energy moves into your house and from room to room along pathways that are either pre-existing or created. It is common for energy to be blocked. This creates dead spaces void of energy in other parts of the house. Energy paths should be open but not so open that the energy cannot be at least momentarily captured and used before it moves on.

Various things block energy flow. The most common are structural walls and furniture. Walls are difficult to move, but there are ways to help move the energy through these spots that we will discuss later in this chapter. An energy blockage caused by furniture, of course, is easily remedied if one knows where to start. Feng shui concepts promote energy flow around furniture so that good energy can invigorate the right places, like conversational areas and creative spaces, or can slow down in places in your home intended for relaxation.

Energy Flowing Too Fast

Not only do you want to be careful not to block energy flow in and around your home, but you want to avoid the opposite too: energy paths so open that ch'i zips right through without hanging around long enough to be used. Again, furniture placement can make all the difference, but other remedies can also help slow down the energy paths inherent in your home's structure.

As Jenny T. Liu says on the *Feng Shui Times* Web site: "Feng Shui is not a quick fix, it is a way of living."

Sometimes energy blocks can be created on purpose. Areas in your home such as window seats, conservatory rooms, and cozy nooks for contemplative pursuits need energy but not the zippy kind of energy you want in more active areas where conversation or artistic creativity is encouraged. Arranging those reflective areas to slow the flow of environmental energy down to the pace of the intended use of the room is important.

Yin and Yang

Before we get into the details of furniture placement, the accessories that help slow down or clear blocked energy, or the use of color and specific elements, it's important to understand yin and yang. These are the terms used to denote balance of opposing values, such as dark and light, warm and cool, angry and sad, or male and female. The yin and yang symbol—the circle composed of intertwined black and white swirls, each dotted with the opposite color—is by now common to most everyone. But the relevance of yin and yang in feng shui practice is no commonplace thing.

Since yin and yang symbolize balance, they get to the heart of all that feng shui is fundamentally about: balancing energy flow to harmonize your environment. For everything, feng shui makes use of a balancing opposite. Always remember this concept, and your own attempts at feng shui will probably work out.

For example, if the ch'i in a room seems too energetic, a common feng shui energy fix is to hang a wind chime or crystal to break energy up. For an inside space, you may not want to hang the crystal or wind chime in the room itself but perhaps in the foyer or the entrance so that some of the energy is deflected to other areas outside the room.

The Five Elements

The Ba-Gua is an energy template that is at the core of feng shui. The five elements of the Ba-Gua underlie the yin/yang principle, but they are not at odds with each other; they are the epitome of those all-important feng shui concepts of balance and harmony of opposites—characteristics like hot and cold, dry and wet.

FACT

There are many Web sites devoted to feng shui. Some offer advice. Others, such as the American Feng Shui Institute (✍ *www.amfengshui.com*) offer online courses at the beginner and intermediate levels. You can also contact them at ▣ 108 North Ynez Ave., Suite 202, Monterey Park, CA 91754.

The five elements of the Ba-Gua are fire, wood, metal, water, and earth. These elements create the dynamic relationship of energy. When a home, room, or space has too much of a certain element, another of these elements can be used to create balance.

The Cycle of Elements

The Ba-Gua's five elements, like everything in nature, have great influence over each other. The destructive cycle starts with wood, which moves earth. Earth blocks water flow; water puts out fire; fire melts metal; and metal cuts wood.

The good news is that there is a creative cycle, too. Fire creates earth in the form of ash; earth creates the minerals that make metal; metal, via condensation, creates water; water cultivates wood; and, completing the cycle, wood is necessary for fire.

You can use these cycles to help you choose the colors of your home, from ceiling to floor, from outside to inside.

Know It Well

The Ba-Gua is represented by an octagonal shape and can be thought of as an energy road map. It can help you figure out the compass directions in your home in which to enhance or downplay a certain element, color, or number in order to influence the key aspect of life that the compass direction controls. If you become captivated by feng shui, the first thing you will want to spend some time understanding is the Ba-Gua.

Using Colors

Color is a key element in decorating according to feng shui principles. Using color successfully is a complex matter. For instance, the color your neighbors choose for their house has great influence on the best color for your house. If a neighbor's house is painted in a color destructive to the color of yours, it will drag down the ch'i of your home.

▲ Keeping a clear pathway is important to good feng shui.

If either house is red, for instance, it will have a dominating effect on any neighboring house painted white. When the color scheme is difficult to change, you can break the influence of your neighbor's house by planting a tree strategically between the houses.

As for the individual rooms in your home, it is no coincidence that primary colors are often first choices for children's areas—these bright, energetic colors are appropriately stimulating for the energy of youth.

Kitchens are thought best to be white—a clean color that offers a neutral backdrop for exhibiting food in colorful dishware. White is also the color of metal on the Ba-Gua Five Elements Color Wheel, which meshes well with the fire predominant in the kitchen.

The Significance of Numbers

Numbers, colors, and compass direction all correspond with the five elements—fire, earth, metal, water, wood—and can all be placed in conjunction or in opposition to each other to good feng shui advantage.

The number nine, for example, corresponds to the compass direction south, whose corresponding color is red and whose element is fire. The four compass points correspond as follows:

Compass direction	Number	Element	Color
north	1	water	black
south	9	fire	red
east	3	wood	green
west	7	metal	white

Of course, there is always the possibility of too much of a good thing. Numbers can help offset this. If you have a kitchen with a southern exposure and red countertops and curtains, that is a lot of fire. You might balance some of that with the opposite—water—by adding a single conspicuous black item that will tone the heat down a little. Just don't get too carried away; water douses fire!

Putting Feng Shui into Practice

How do you get started making use of feng shui in your own home? First, you need to ask some basic questions to begin assessing the current status of energy flow and harmonizing balance in your home.

What to Look For

Start with the entrance to your home and consider how inviting and auspicious it makes your home appear. No matter where the entry, how grand or how modest, good feng shui is important here.

Are there easily recognizable "dead spaces" in your home, such as areas where hallways converge or blank walls? These will need some ch'i redirecting.

Is one area particularly susceptible to collecting clutter? A hanging crystal can help clear up some dull energy here.

Do you awake feeling rested and energized? Is your bedroom tranquil and conducive to sleep? Avoid clutter in the bedroom and pick restful colors, where good ch'i can linger but not bounce around the room making it too energetic for rest.

FACT

If you are looking for a wide range of feng shui accoutrements but don't have a feng shui store in your vicinity, visit the Feng Shui Emporium at ✍ *www.fengshuiemporium.com*. There you will find crystals, incense burners, bamboo flutes, wind chimes, a wide variety of mirrors, and more, complete with photos and descriptions.

If you have a home office and/or work from home, are work and good projects coming in? Bills being paid? Are you able to succeed with the projects you get? Moving the office to the wealth sector of the southeast compass point and/or adding some of the wealth color—purple—might help.

Is your kitchen a place where you enjoy preparing meals, where cooking feels creative? White is the best color for the kitchen and uncluttered, clean cooking space is critical. In many homes, the stove placement puts the cook's back to the kitchen doorway; if that's the case, add a mirror so you can cook without being surprised from behind.

Every room in your home can benefit from feng shui changes, from the bathroom to the living room to the bedroom. If you and your spouse find you are arguing a lot these days, perhaps the color scheme in the kitchen makes the area where you cook your meals, already laden with heat, too hot. Change a couple of colors, hang a mirror, and see what happens!

What to Look Out For

Here are some basics that represent good and bad feng shui. Try following these, which will help you get the idea of what other things you can enhance in your home:

- Furniture with sharp corners and jutting walls that create sharp corners are considered "poison arrows." Be careful these things do not aim at critical places like your bed, dining table, or front door.

- Keep toilet lids closed. Water is wealth, and an open lid is said to allow wealth to flush right out of the home.
- Electronic equipment gives off electromagnetic fields. It should not be present in rooms whose primary purpose is peace and tranquility, such as the bedroom.
- Keep your home's entryway in good repair and attractive and inviting to positive ch'i. Repaint weathered doors, replace light bulbs, and landscape attractively around your entry.

QUESTION?

What if there are "bad" feng shui elements that can't be moved?
Think nature. Use indoor fountains to enhance ch'i, and use plants to create a soft and natural environment. The natural world is fundamental to feng shui. You won't go too far wrong if you try to cure your home's ills by using balms from nature.

The Ba-Gua's Energy Map

The Ba-Gua's energy map shows how energy flows through our physical world. To bring harmony and balance into your life, use this map to match the energy in your home to the different energetic patterns represented by the different sectors of the Ba-Gua. To do this, you'll first need to map the Ba-Gua onto your home, starting with your front doorway, so you know which areas of your home relate to which sectors.

In traditional Buddhist feng shui, the front door is *always* the mouth of chi (where the energy enters the home). Looking at the Ba-Gua energy map, you'll notice that you will always enter the home in one of three different sectors. Standing outside looking toward the door, it will be in either knowledge/spirituality to the left, career/life path in the center, or helpful people/travel to the right.

Picture your home as a big square or rectangle or even a tic-tac-toe board that divides your home into nine equal sections. Now align the Ba-Gua with your front door. If your front door is in the center of your home (like many center-hall colonials) then you'd be entering in the career sector of your home and the other sectors would follow suit accordingly.

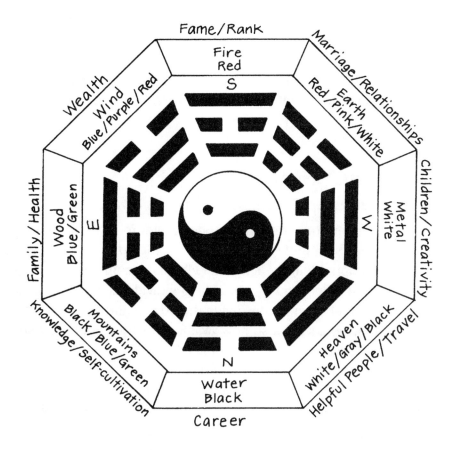

Fame/Rank

Fire
Red
S

Marriage/Relationships

Wealth

Wind
Blue/Purple/Red

Earth
Red/Pink/White

Children/Creativity

Family/Health

Wood
Blue/Green
E

Metal
White
W

Knowledge/Self-cultivation

Mountains
Black/Blue/Green

Heaven
White/Gray/Black

Helpful People/Travel

N

Water
Black

Career

▲ The Ba-Gua energy map can help you determine which areas of your home relate to which feng shui sectors.

Feng Shui Fixes

Don't despair if you feel like your home is just a feng shui disaster. There are many things that can be addressed and fixed to change the feng shui in your home. Here are a few ideas:

- Use mirrors and crystals to break up and redirect energy blockages or to deflect bad energy away from an area. Mirrors are even suggested for outside, to deflect negative energy from a neighbor.
- Plants and folding screens are also used extensively in feng shui

to block poison daggers and soften effects of bad feng shui.

- Wealth and water go hand in hand. Add an aquarium or fountain to your home office to help cash flow with the water.
- Red and the compass direction south are the prime luck factors in feng shui. Red front doors facing south are thought to be of the highest luck.

Professional Help

Our homes are of utmost importance to us. As the application of feng shui in interior home design has become more recognized in this country, feng shui professionals are cropping up in all parts of the United States. Also prevalent are feng shui classes at community colleges, health centers, and other venues, which help individuals put the principles into practice in their own homes using the advice and guidance of a professional. Many books are also now available that focus on feng shui and provide detailed instruction on topics that may be specific to your home.

A lot of feng shui is based on logic. Even if you can't go the distance with your belief in some of the cosmic principles, these logical applications of feng shui make sense. If your budget can stand the hiring of a feng shui practitioner and there is someone available in your area, that's great! If that's not possible, perhaps there is a feng shui class within commuting distance where you can get some solid advice and background to make some changes in your home yourself.

Feng shui is just one more way to help make our homes the nourishing, comforting, enjoyable places we want them to be.

Finding a local feng shui practitioner could be difficult. Click on the Feng Shui Guild's Web site at ✍ *www.fengshuiguild.com*, and you will find a state-by-state listing of feng shui practitioners. The listings include addresses, phone numbers, e-mail addresses, and Web sites (where applicable). The Guild also offers a newsletter and has listings of feng shui schools and local Feng Shui Guild chapters.

Chapter 6
Ceilings

You might think at the beginning of your project, "The ceiling looks fine." But once you apply fresh paint to the walls, your ceiling will start to look dirty and dull before the first coat of wall paint is even dry. Address the ceiling before you start anything else in the room. In practice, you will want to implement your decorating plan from the ceiling down.

Drywall

Even if your intention is simply to freshen up a room, if there is some ceiling damage, you will want to take the time to repair it so that the remainder of your redecorating job will look its best. Drywall may be the most common material you encounter in ceilings and walls, at least in houses built since its introduction in the 1940s. This product, which comes in sheets like plywood (typically measuring four foot by eight), can be incredibly easy to work with when it is on the wall. But repairing or replacing ceiling drywall can be a bit trickier.

ALERT!

If you need to replace the whole ceiling—a renovation project more than a decorating project—you will almost certainly want to hire a professional. Sheets of drywall are heavy and cumbersome. Professionals have all the special tools that make working with something like this much easier, and they have the experience to help them get through the touchy parts.

Patching Drywall

Patching drywall is a little more within the range of the do-it-yourself crowd, although you won't encounter many damaged areas in drywall ceilings. Drywall patches usually fix damage caused by things like a door that didn't have a doorstop, whose handle pushed through the wall, or other accidental holes. In the ceiling, the most common time you will need a patch is when you replace a light fixture. If this case, be certain to turn off the circuit to the light before you patch the area around it.

If you are replacing the fixture altogether and the existing hole is too large for the new fixture, you'll do best to pull the fixture out and create a patch that will fill in the gap as if you were going to leave the ceiling clear without a light. Then, before you place the patch, drill a hole for the electrical line to come through the ceiling.

If the new light is a heavy fixture, it might be tough to hang it on a patched area. Move the overhead light to an area away from the patch if at all possible.

To patch drywall, you will need these tools:

- Utility knife
- Tape measure
- Straight edge
- Joint compound
- Drywall tape
- Wide putty knife
- Sheet or half-sheet of drywall, depending on the size of your patch

How to Do It

Cut the damaged area with the utility knife to create a square hole. Make the edges even by cutting with a straightedge. Measure the hole carefully. Cut your patch from the piece of drywall, taking care to *cut 2 inches wider on all sides than the hole.* Drywall has a paper backing, and you want to leave a border of that backing to help hold the drywall patch on. Cut away the stiff part of the 2-inch border, leaving the paper backing.

You may want to drill a hole for your electrical line at this point, before the patch goes on the ceiling. Coat the paper backing with joint cement and place the patch in the hole, paper backing side out. Use the putty knife to smooth the backing onto the ceiling and squeeze out any excess joint compound to leave it flat. Let this dry for twenty-four hours or so, then coat the edges of the patch with another layer of joint compound, trying to make it smooth and blend in with the surrounding drywall as well as possible. Be careful with this stage—paint will cover some of the unevenness, but the smoother you can get the edges, the more the patch will blend into its surroundings.

FACT

Drywall is often referred to as Sheetrock, but Sheetrock is actually a brand name. Drywall is also often called gypsum wallboard, gypsum being one of the main products used to make the sheet of drywall. It can get confusing!

Plaster

If your house was built before 1950, chances are pretty good that the ceilings are made of plaster. If it's even older, the plaster will probably be horsehair plaster—horsehair was mixed with the other plaster materials to hold it all together.

When patching plaster ceilings, you are usually dealing with cracks. Don't let yourself be tempted to skip the patching work and paint over cracks. They will show through immediately, and if they begin to fall apart even more, they will crumble into your paint and on the brush or roller and really make a mess.

To patch a small crack, oddly enough, you will first need to make it bigger. But in a ceiling, you need to be careful to make it only a little bigger since the larger the crack the more patching plaster you will need. The plaster is heavy, so the more you need, the more chance it will sag from the ceiling. Of course, it is possible to do a big patching job in a plaster ceiling, but it is one of those things best left up to professionals.

Here are the steps to patching plaster ceilings:

1. Dig out along the crack line with a chisel and small hammer.
2. Bevel the edges of the crack, going wider toward the inside of the crack. This will help the crack to hold the patching plaster.
3. If the crack is pretty narrow—¼ inch or so—you can use a premixed patching material. These usually come in a plastic container with a resealable lid and can also be used for patching drywall and other materials. If the crack is any wider, you will need to use patching plaster that comes as a powder and must be mixed with water. This is not as heavy as the premixed stuff and will hold better in larger areas.
4. If you are using the premixed product, pick up a gob on a putty knife and push it into the crack. Do this all along the crack and keep filling until the crack is full. Scrape it level with the putty knife.
5. Let it dry for twenty-four hours or so, then do it again in order to fill in any part that has sunken in the drying process. Level it off, let it dry, then sand it flat. Wipe the sand off, and you are ready to paint!
6. If you're using patching plaster, the process is not much different. If the crack is pretty wide, you may need to fill it in layers, at least two, maybe three. The crack should be wide enough and completely cleaned out down to the lathe (the wooden boards under the plaster that the plaster adheres to). Apply your first layer to the lathe; don't worry about smoothing it off, you want the surface to be rough so

that the next layer will adhere to it better.

7. Once it's dry, apply the next layer. You may even need to apply a third layer depending on how wide and thick the crack is. Once it is full and level with its surroundings, lightly sand it to smooth it out.

Once these patches are painted over with a couple of coats of ceiling paint, they won't be noticeable at all! You should be able to use any standard ceiling paint on a plaster ceiling, but always check the label to make sure the paint is suitable for the material you are putting it on.

A roller extension is a useful gadget that will make painting easier and make the job look more professional. Roller extensions come in different sizes, and they screw into the regular handle of a paint roller. These aren't just handy—they can help with safety as well, enabling you to paint the ceiling without having to be on a ladder.

Dropped Ceilings

Chances are you won't do much with a dropped ceiling when you are doing a decorating project. Typically, these ceilings consist of a plastic or metal grid dropped from the original ceiling. Placed in the grid are panels of ceiling material (usually in very manageable sizes, around two by four feet) that typically have the advantage of offering some acoustical properties. This material is often very lightweight. It is easy to take in and out of the grid. You simply push the panel up into the empty space above it, tilt the panel, and pull it out.

Dropped ceilings are usually installed to cover a badly damaged ceiling that the previous owner (or possibly the current owner, if you are renting) chose not to repair, probably to save the time and expense such a project would require. If you decide it's time to take on the job yourself, you are now going way beyond a decorating project! But it may be worth it to make an extensive decorating effort look its best.

One feature that is common with dropped ceilings is that to offer overall lighting, a few panels in the ceiling are often translucent plastic that cover fluorescent bulbs. Depending on the use of the room, this may be just the thing you need. However, ambient fluorescent lighting is often not the best way to show off your new decorating scheme. You could simply not use the lights and include enough task lighting in your new decorating plan to make up for the light. You might choose to replace the translucent panels with ceiling panels, but it may be hard to match the rest of the ceiling—the old and new panels may be slightly different shades of white, and it may be difficult to fit in regular panels with the light fixture above them. Or you could choose to keep the lighting but to soften it by replacing glaring white fluorescent bulbs with soft-light fluorescents.

Tin Ceilings

A decorative tin ceiling is probably the most eye-catching of all ceilings, excepting perhaps one painted like the Sistine Chapel. Tin ceilings, a common decorative element in the Victorian era, can be installed like dropped ceilings to cover up damage to an existing ceiling. They are especially appropriate for late nineteenth- and early twentieth-century houses.

Tin ceiling tiles are still readily available to purchase new. Check the magazines listed in Appendix A for available patterns. They usually come in panels made up of several 12-inch squares of the pattern.

ALERT!

If your home has a vintage tin ceiling, you may want to consult a restoration expert about how to clean it.

Tin ceilings can be painted. Be sure to use an oil-based paint as a water-based paint will cause the tin to rust. In the kitchen, where grease may accumulate more readily on a tin ceiling, you can clean it with mineral spirits and coat it with lacquer to help deter the grease.

Exposed Beams

If your home is of a Colonial era and style, there may already be rooms where the ceiling beams were exposed or were never covered to begin with. Back in the early days of home building, the expense of covering post-and-beam structural elements was left to the wealthy or at best the more formal rooms in the home. After all, the colonists were not able to run down to the nearest warehouse home store and look through dozens of wallpaper books and change decorating schemes as often as we do now.

Decorating around Exposed Beams

Exposed beams present some significant decorating considerations. First, if the room is one that you wish to be formal, do not expose the beams if they aren't already. If they are exposed, you may want to consider covering them with drywall to give the room a more formal atmosphere.

◀ Angled ceilings and dramatic arches give this bathroom a very regal feel.

If the room is intended to be more rustic, exposed beams can be just the thing. In older homes, the beams are just fascinating to ponder—how they were milled and got to where they now are placed is hard to grasp! They were typically hand-milled from trees that were growing right on the property. There are clues that tell how the beams were created—signs and characteristics that are recognizable by preservation and restoration experts. Identifying the techniques that were used is a good way to help date a house's original construction.

Doing It Yourself

You may decide to expose beams yourself. This is not a difficult task, but it is usually quite a dirty one. You'll need to totally clear the room. The ceiling material itself, whether drywall or plaster, will be messy. But what you won't know until it is coming down is what is lurking between the ceiling and the bottom of the upper floor; mice could have been having years of celebrations with stored corn cobs and nesting material in the void.

When you are deciding whether or not to expose beams, keep in mind that it will have a great deal of influence on the remainder of the room's décor. Dark walls, either painted or wallpapered, may have been fine with a white plaster or drywall ceiling, but once the beams are exposed the whole room becomes darker. Unless the room has lots of windows or is a room that you want to be dark and cozy, you may want to consider lighter walls.

FACT

Better Homes and Gardens has a highly searchable Web site at *www.bhg.com*. It is full of step-by-step simple projects for the ambitious do-it-yourselfer and lots of decorating ideas and pictures.

In decorating wish-books, you will often see rustic exposed beams littered with baskets. If baskets are your thing, then go for it. But if you are considering hanging baskets from the beams just because it seems like the thing to do for the era and style, go easy on the numbers. Buy handmade baskets of high quality craftsmanship and interesting design; the fewer you have, the more attention each lovely work of art will get.

Lighting fixtures will also need special consideration. They are discussed in more detail in Chapter 10.

Dressing It up with Molding

Ceilings can be dressed up by installing a crown molding along the upper edge of the wall. The molding should probably match the style of your home—the Colonial era, if it had such embellishments at all, would have had very simple ones, while a Victorian-style home would have been full of ornate architectural elements such as elegant crown molding.

Molding between the ceiling and the wall can also help hide uneven edges and give either paint or wallpaper a more polished look, always a plus after you work so hard to decorate.

Colored Ceilings?

It is certainly possible to paint your ceiling a color. Ceiling paint is not special paint, just flat white paint, usually latex like most paints these days. Flat paint is less reflective and ceiling paints are standard white because paint tends to dry darker than what you see in the can. Dark paints make the ceiling seem lower and therefore the room seem smaller. However, if you want to paint your ceiling a color other than white, you can have flat white ceiling paint tinted with standard paint tinting mixtures.

A common ceiling problem is discoloration due to a leaky roof or a bathroom on the story above. First and foremost, fix the leak. Regular ceiling paint will not cover leak stains. It may look like it does while you are painting, but as soon as the paint dries, the stain will begin to show through. Use a product, such as one called Bin, to cover up the stain before painting the ceiling—Bin is simply painted on like regular paint. Painting ceilings is hard work. Take advantage of this simple fix to make your hard work look polished.

However, other rooms can certainly enjoy the element of surprise of a nonwhite ceiling, especially if the room is large and the ceiling is high. Coral, blue, and other elegant colors can very nicely show off a Victorian-style white ceiling medallion (described in the next section).

Ceiling Decorations

If there is a common ceiling decoration, a medallion is probably it. Ceiling medallions are usually specifically used with light fixtures. They are rarely installed today but, hey, why not do something different?

If you are attempting to bring down a ceiling but do not want to go to great extents to do that, you can try draping fabric to create a false ceiling. You'll want to use something light and airy and probably transparent unless you are also trying to cover up a particularly unattractive ceiling.

ALERT!

Don't paint around ceiling fans and light fixtures; take the time to remove them before you start to paint. Keep track of how all the pieces came apart—not just the electrical fittings, but the way the whole fixture connected to the ceiling and the parts to each other—so you can easily put them back together. And don't forget: As with any other time you work with electrical fixtures, *turn the power to the fixture off* before you start to unscrew anything.

Ceiling Fans

The ceiling decoration we see most often these days is something that is also practical: the ceiling fan. Ceiling fans are not just for cooling. They are also very helpful in circulating heat around a room with a high ceiling, in which the warm air floats to the top and does little for the comfort of the room's occupants.

Ceiling fans, which are typically equipped with lights, are covered in more detail in Chapter 10. It seems logical to get a ceiling fan with at least one light even if you don't feel the room needs more light. However, if the height of the room is a consideration or you just don't want the look of a ceiling fan with a light, there are many styles available that are just fans and nothing more.

Ceiling fans have become so popular that they are available in many styles, from the traditional paddle fan with the caned blades to high-tech metal fans with long extenders.

Chapter 7

Walls

The walls of your home are the largest expanse that you will be dealing with when it comes to decorating. You can do a lot to a wall, and that's before you ever even think about hanging decorative items like artwork or antiques from it. This chapter covers the basics, including a description of the materials walls are made of and techniques of painting and wallpapering.

What Walls Are Made Of

Before you decide what you might want to cover—or, more often, re-cover—them with, you will first want to assess what material your walls are made of. The two most common materials you will run across, as with ceilings, are plaster and drywall. If your house was built after the 1950s, chances are slim that you will have plaster walls. Drywall had become incredibly popular by then. The ease with which it could be installed, the relative cost compared to plaster, and the appeal of square corners and level walls quickly eclipsed plaster as a wall-building material. Plaster walls began to come back into vogue after the 1960s, during the old home revival movement, when people started to appreciate the richness and stability of older materials.

Of course, there are other things you may run into besides plaster and drywall. Many kitchen and bathroom walls make use of ceramic tile and linoleum-like products—which are usually installed over drywall or plaster anyway—but in your redecorating effort, you will be dealing mostly with the surface material. The kitchen and bathroom, where cleaning is a big issue, made ready use of tile and linoleum, which are easily cleaned. Removing and replacing large expanses of ceramic tile is a much bigger job than what we generally define as a decorating project! However, installing a few tiles above the kitchen or bathroom sink can be a small project that gives you dramatic results.

To remove wallpaper, especially wallpaper that has been painted over, you will want to score the surface first to allow whatever stripping agent you use—even if it's just plain water—to get below the wallpaper to the glue. If you just spray the product on top of the painted wallpaper, it won't help loosen the glue much, if at all.

You may also encounter paneling over basically nothing, tacked onto strapping and the framing two-by-fours. If the paneling is on an outside wall, there is probably at least some insulation in between.

You may also encounter walls that you thought were simply painted, but on closer inspection you find that the paint job was actually done over wallpaper. In a case like this, you will need to choose whether to remove the wallpaper or simply paint another coat over the existing paint. If you are just freshening up the room, it's probably fine to paint on another coat. However, if you are doing an extensive decorating job that you plan to have last for several years, you should go ahead and actually strip the wallpaper off and the old paint job along with it. It may not be as difficult as it seems up front—water-based latex paints can often help lift the wallpaper paste from the wall surface, making the stripping job a little easier.

Again, removing and replacing walls is a major project. In redecorating a room, on the other hand, incorporating a new wall paint color or wallpaper design adds a key decorating element to any room. You need to know what you are starting with.

Working with Plaster Walls

Plaster is easily painted over or covered with wallpaper, but the thing to keep in mind with plaster is that it will almost definitely require some patching and repair work before you start covering it. You don't need to be a master craftsman in order to make small plaster repairs. It is relatively easy to work with, and plaster walls tend to be uneven and a bit rough anyway. Small repairs that aren't perfectly smooth won't be out of place, and they probably won't even be noticeable once you've painted or papered and hung things on the wall. So don't ignore those cracks and divots. Go ahead and patch them before you get started.

Getting wallpaper off plaster is fairly easy. Plaster tends to be damp, and older wallpaper often peels right off it in sheets. That's because over the years, the dampness of the plaster has helped the wallpaper paste begin to lift from the wall.

Working with Drywall Walls

You may need to spend a little time patching drywall (also called gypsum wallboard or Sheetrock) as well. The tubs of premixed patching that we use these days for small plaster patches is the same stuff you'll use for drywall. Patches in drywall are much more noticeable because the rest of the wall, by nature, is pretty even. But don't worry, it's also easy to make the patches even as well.

Buy a tub of the patching compound and a small trowel or putty knife at your local hardware or home improvement store and follow the directions on the tub. Spend the time to sink and cover nail heads that have come loose as well. These simple repairs are worth it; if you are going to spend time freshening the room up, you want the job to look finished when you are done.

FACT

If you wish your home had more architectural details from the period it was built, you can always add them. There are architectural salvage stores across the country that buy up pieces that have been removed from people's homes or from homes that are being destroyed. Some of the salvage stores have Web sites, including these: Architectural Salvage Inc. in Brentwood, NH (✎ *www.oldhousesalvage.com*); Olde Good Things Architectural Antiques and Artifacts (✎ *www.ogtstore.com*); and Architectural Salvage Warehouse, 🖳 53 Main Street, Burlington, VT 05401. These companies offer huge pieces like mantels, columns, and posts in addition to plumbing fixtures and small hardware items.

Walls of Wood

Warm, natural-toned wood walls tend toward a casual look. White painted paneled doors help create a more elegant look. The wood interior of a log cabin is quite rustic. Wainscoting below plaster or drywall creates a great space for hanging pictures and wall art on the wall above. However, wainscoting can be a little restrictive when it comes to high furnishings. It can make them seem a bit busy and keep them from sitting flush against the wall.

Color Choices

Once you've determined what your walls are made of—and keep in mind that you may have plaster in most rooms and drywall in the addition—you will want to think about color. The information on color in Chapter 4 will help in this decision, but the color of your walls is such an important consideration that we'll cover a few things here as well.

▲ Boldly patterned wallpapers give this room a cozy, welcoming feel.

Bold or Understated?

To decorate the walls of a room, decide first if there is a wall that is a natural focal point for the room—a wall of windows or a fireplace, with or without a prominent mantel, would be an obvious choice. However, there might be other things to notice as well. Where does your eye fall when you walk into the room? Do you plan to make a part of the room a conversation area? You can make the wall behind this area a fitting backdrop and a natural focal point regardless of whether there's a fireplace or dramatic view there or not. A piece of art, lighting, stenciling, textured wallpaper, or a striking piece of furniture like a highboy or grandfather clock all serve this purpose. Give the room focus and let the eye settle, not drift around from floor to ceiling and place to place.

The Color White

The old standby color is, of course, some shade of white. White is never a bad choice—even if you are discouraged with yourself that you are more traditional than you thought, white offers a neutral palette for getting bold with your accessories. White walls allow you to easily incorporate bold colors in the form of pottery, artwork, and even plants with brightly colored flowers.

Bright or Dark Colors

Although your friends and family may make faces when you tell them you are painting your living room walls dark blue or your dining room yellow, don't be afraid to use a bold wall color. It is a little tougher to paint over, but if you decide you don't like it after a while, it can be painted over with a coat of primer and a couple of coats of lighter paint.

ALERT!

Artwork can be a focal point or an accent, but don't clutter the walls with so many pictures scattered about that the eye doesn't know where to settle first. If you want to hang numerous pictures, consider framing similar themes with similar frames and grouping them to make a more dynamic impact.

Don't, however, be too quick to jump to conclusions as you are painting or wallpapering. When it is bare and covered with drop cloths, you see nothing but this bold color you've chosen. But once the whole job is done and your walls are decorated with carefully chosen accent pieces, the room will look quite different!

If the room is one you entertain in, you will be rewarded for your choice with comments from your guests on how dramatic or elegant or bright the room looks. If it's a room that guests do not go in, then you can feel more free to do whatever you want anyway.

Wallpaper

The array of wallpaper available to the home decorator can be a bit overwhelming. Even small hardware stores carry wallpaper books galore. However, choosing wallpaper can be made more fun instead of daunting if you consider some things before you go to look through books.

Choosing Your Pattern

Do you want the wallpaper to have a bold pattern that dominates the room and creates a strong decorating statement all on its own? Or do you want the wallpaper to blend into the background more with a small repeating pattern that doesn't overpower the art and other pieces you will be hanging on the walls of the room? Pattern and dominant color are two important choices you can make before you ever start looking at specific papers. Making these decisions can help to easily eliminate choices as you flip through the dozens of books, each with dozens of wallpaper samples.

ESSENTIAL

Don't hesitate to let the clerk in the wallpaper section help you. He or she has probably come to know different manufacturers and what their specialties are, and can point you in a direction that will save you some time (and brain power!) looking.

Choose a day when you have some time to look at papers. Once you get to the store, you'll find that the wallpaper manufacturers themselves have helped to organize your choices. They not only have broken their sample books down into papers typical for different rooms of the home, but the manufacturers often have specialties when it comes to style. You'll find books with classic country styles, traditional styles, floral patterns, or papers for kids' rooms.

Lastly, start the search process as soon as you can after deciding you are going to paper. You may find wallpaper that is in stock, but it is also possible that the paper you love must be ordered and takes three weeks to arrive. You don't want to hear that if you've already prepared all your walls and planned to have had the room papered by next Saturday, when you are entertaining important guests. Then you'd have to settle for what's in stock. With the wide range of wallpaper offerings, it would be unfortunate to limit your choices this way.

The Wallpapering Process

The actual installation of wallpaper can be both easy and difficult. If you plan to have a professional do it, then your time can be spent making the choice of pattern. You can also plan to hang the paper yourself. It is not a difficult thing to do, for the most part, but you'll want to have the right tools on hand to make the job easier.

Any store that sells wallpaper will have an array of tools that can help make the final job look professional. Prepare the walls before you get set up to paper.

Here are the basic steps involved in the wallpapering process:

- Start papering on one corner of the room and work your way around the room clockwise.
- Follow the carpenter's and seamstress's adage: "Measure twice, cut once." Be sure to consider the wallpaper's pattern and match the pattern carefully. The more often a pattern repeats in the paper, the less wallpaper you will waste.
- When hanging long pieces of wallpaper, fold the bottom back onto itself (don't crease, just roll), glue side onto glue side, to shorten the piece for easier handling. Adhere the top portion in place on the wall and then carefully unfold the bottom and adhere that. Although you want to be careful while handling wet wallpaper, it is not quite as delicate as you might think. Once it's on the wall, you can still slide it around a bit to butt it up against the piece before it.
- Smaller pieces are certainly easier to handle than larger pieces, but they can be fussier to cut. You can always cut long and use a straight

edge and utility knife to cut the top and bottom edges to fit. However, you'll need an extremely sharp blade, and you will not be able to cut the damp paper evenly.

Don't sidestep the prep work on walls. After putting the time, money, and energy into redecorating a room to the extent of putting new paint or paper on the walls, you don't want to be discouraged by the blemishes that could have been easily patched ahead of time.

Borders

Wallpaper borders have come a long way in terms of selection. Almost every wallpaper book now has a section of borders at the front. Borders often coordinate with wallpaper designs, but that doesn't mean they have to be used together. A wallpaper border can also bring a little extra pizzazz to a painted wall.

Don't feel like you have to put them just at the top of the wall. A border can also look nice when placed flush above a chair rail. As a standalone, a border can actually simulate a chair rail itself.

Die-cut borders are also popular—if the pattern is reversible, you can choose to put the flat edge up or down.

Painting

Painting is one of the easiest things you can do to create a dramatic effect in any room and freshen up a wall in a small amount of time. Here are some tips on painting:

- Be sure to prepare the walls and cover up the floor and any furnishings. Wear clothes you don't mind getting paint on. If you are going to use a roller, cover your hair—it will get splattered!
- Use water-based latex paints for the easiest cleanup.

- Believe the clerk at the paint store. The color in the can will dry darker on the wall.
- Paint the ceiling first, then the walls, and the trim last.
- When painting large expanses, work in sections by rolling an "X" on the wall about two feet wide and three feet high. Begin to fill in the X by rolling vertically and horizontally down and across the middle. Then fill in the whole area and start with a new X until you have done the entire wall.
- Use the handy tools available for edging and keeping paint off other surfaces. They make the job look more professional and you will get less frustrated.
- Use the very best brushes you can afford. It really does make a difference. Likewise with rollers—use good ones, and buy the right nap for the type of surface you are painting.

FACT

To "cut into" window frames and other tight areas, buy a high-quality paintbrush that has a chiseled edge designed to reach into these places. It can be fairly easily done without having to spend time taping the edges with masking tape or coordinating using an edging tool, but you need the right brush and a steady hand.

Special Paint Techniques

Special paint techniques like sponging and marbleizing are simple to do. These styles go in and out of vogue. If you like the look, go ahead with it despite whatever the prevailing fad may be. It can always easily be painted or papered over. That said, it's also a good idea to use these techniques sparingly. They tend to be rather busy by nature, and you can definitely have too much of a good thing. Since they are rather fun to do, it can be tempting to go overboard. If you really like a technique, consider not doing the walls but instead getting it in smaller doses. One way is to apply the look to a piece of furniture that will show up nicely against a plain painted wall.

Sponging

Sponging is easy to do. First you paint the surface a plain color, and then you use a sponge to dab on tinted glaze. The hardest part is deciding what color to use. (You will probably want to test out your color combinations and technique on a sample board first to see how it will look.) The added plus of sponge painting is that it can hide many a flaw. It is a great backdrop for artwork with plain frames.

▲ Special painting techniques can include wall murals such as this one, where a stone archway and palm trees painted on the wall bring some of the outdoors inside.

Marbleizing

Like sponging, marbleizing is a great cover-up for walls that are less than perfect. This technique, however, is a little more complex than sponging, although ultimately it is quite simple. Basically, you are trying to mimic a natural pattern. There are many books available that can guide you through the step-by-step techniques for using this creative paint method.

FACT

For an old-fashioned look, use old-fashioned milk paint, which is made literally from milk (plus water, earth pigments, and lime). One company that sells milk paint is the Old Fashioned Milk Paint Company, ⌨436 Main Street, Groton, MA 01450, telephone ✆ (978) 448-6336; on the Web at ✐ *www.milkpaint.com*. Available in many colors, it is environmentally safe and nontoxic when dry.

Other Techniques

There are also many other paint techniques suitable for walls, such as antiquing and spatter painting. Any good paint store or paint section that sells glaze and tint will have ideas and instructions. Don't be afraid to experiment. Paint techniques like sponging and marbleizing are great ways to blend rooms that are visible from one to the other. You can use opposite colors, painting the base coat in one room the color you use for the technique in the other. Or you can use complementary or neutral colors to create a nice segue from a room painted yellow through a corridor to a room painted blue. Ⓔ

Chapter 8
Floors

At first glance, floors may not seem like much of a consideration when it comes to decorating. In truth, however, floors are second in importance only to walls in terms of the expanse they provide that will serve as a backdrop for your home's décor. If that doesn't make them important enough, they also deserve some amount of your decorating concern on their own account.

Floor Basics

What your floors are made of is an important consideration in planning the decorating and furnishings for the rooms in your home. Ideally, the floors in high-traffic areas, such as kitchens, hallways, and family rooms, are of resilient materials that are easy to clean and keep clean. Wood is not only a perennial favorite for its looks, but it also handles well under wear and tear if maintained properly and, perhaps, is protected by rugs in extra high traffic areas. But the synthetic materials available also hold up well and are quite attractive in their own right.

Wood Floors

The country home absolutely has to have wood floors, at least in some rooms. Country style has come to accommodate almost anything, but wood floors just make perfect stages for country décor and furniture, as well as braided and hooked rugs. Look through the rungs of a Windsor or Shaker style ladderback chair, and you just expect to see wood on the other side.

Soft woods, such as pine, can get roughed up in areas heavily traveled or from pets' sharp claws or high-heeled shoes. But that doesn't have to discourage you. Wear is part of a wood floor's charm. For the most part, the soft woods hold up better than one might first imagine. Take the opportunity to display great area carpets in those places that will receive the most wear and tear, such as under the table, in the entryway, and at doorways. Protect the floor with regular vacuuming to get rid of dirt that can grind into the wood and its finish.

ALERT!

If you are not much for vacuuming and regular cleaning, avoid high maintenance floors like cork. It's a shame to ruin your beautiful decorating with a dusty, dirty, scuffed backdrop.

If you set plant pots on a wood floor, use trays or dishes or some sort of protective container that prevents the moisture from the pot from leaving white moisture stains on waxed floors. Be careful when watering the plants not to splash water or overflow the container.

Things that won't move, such as crocks, large pottery, or stationary furniture like bookcases and end tables, don't need much in the way of protection. Furniture that gets scraped across the floor, on the other hand, needs to be set on carpets or to have protective rubber tips or leg pads attached. This is to keep the floor from getting constantly scratched and is especially necessary for chairs and sofas that regularly get the extra weight of a person added to them.

Wood floors can always be refinished. While it isn't a job you want to have to do annually or even semiannually, buffing up and resurfacing your wood floors once every five to ten years is not an impossible job.

Synthetic Materials

Laminates have become not only more popular, but they have also become increasingly attractive over the last twenty years. They can often be easily installed by an ambitious do-it-yourself homeowner since they typically come in squares or strips and are laid down in piecemeal fashion. The hardest part is dealing first with the preparation of the surface that they will go on. With the latest technology, you really can get a wood appearance and a sturdy feel from these products.

Laminates have a protective layer on their surface, known as the "image layer." This is the layer that projects the wood image you are seeking. Underneath that is a core layer, which is the backing of the image layer, and the laminate itself. With the concern over environmental hazards, glueless products are also coming onto the market.

Rolled linoleum is also always a popular choice. Styles and patterns have become increasingly sophisticated, although the color schemes and designs of the early to mid-twentieth century are now considered almost objects of art. Linoleum was once popular for retro-style decorating, but recently there have been many small companies that are restoring old linoleum into smaller scatter carpets.

The color choices available today are endless and can fit any décor. They are easy to clean, easy to maintain, and they withstand lots of abuse. Typically available rolled, you can also get linoleum squares and piece together a floor patchwork as easily as squares and strips of wood laminate.

Flooring that is embossed with a three-dimensional texture can be leveled with a compound that then allows you to install new flooring right over it.

Carpets

Wall-to-wall carpet is often the flooring of choice in apartments, suburban homes, and many other new homes. From a practical standpoint, carpeting offers warmth and consistency of style throughout the home. With many exceptions, of course, these newer homes don't typically contain the same types of architectural details and wood floors that older homes do. Instead, a rough subfloor is laid, and a wall-to-wall carpet gets installed over it.

If you have wall-to-wall carpeting in an older home, you probably will find a well-preserved wood floor underneath it. Some people do find wood floors intimidating and prefer to cover them up. If you're thinking of tearing out wall-to-wall carpet that is in great condition, think carefully about the job you might be getting in for. Are you really ready to tear up perfectly good flooring if it means facing the possibility that the wood floor underneath needs lots of work?

FACT

Great care should be taken of antique and old carpets. Use carpet pads underneath them. Turn them regularly, and use casters under furniture legs and rubber tips on chair legs that will rest on them. Vacuum at least weekly.

If the carpet simply doesn't suit your decorating needs, then by all means start pulling it up! If it's a shag rug, then unless you are planning to decorate in 1970s style with lava lamps and Naugahyde-covered furniture, get the shag out of the house! But if the carpet is not stained or worn, and you think you could live with it for a couple of years, you may want to spend your time and money elsewhere for the time being.

Floors Room by Room

The pros and cons of different flooring options are discussed in detail in the chapters on each individual room. We'll discuss them briefly here as well because a choice of floors requires you to take so many practical considerations into account, in addition to personal taste. Choosing flooring for a particular room requires careful consideration of questions like the kind of use, wear, and tear that will be foisted upon it.

As we've discussed before with decorating consistency throughout the house, it is certainly possible that all the floors in your home are not the same. It can be a good decorating move to establish a sense of consistency from room to room, especially in those rooms that are visible from each other. However, sometimes just the opposite effect is best, and you can use differences in floor treatment to really set off one room from another.

In the Kitchen

In almost every home, the kitchen is a high-traffic area. Even if the most-used entrance doesn't dump into the kitchen, which it often does, the kitchen gets traffic from meal preparation several times a day plus those endless trips by everyone in the family to the refrigerator and the sink.

Carpeting in the kitchen is rare, but scatter rugs at the places where someone is likely to stand for lengths of time is nice. A soft rug at the sink and one near the stove makes a nice place for the chef or the dishwasher to rest his or her feet. These will be subject to spills and splatters and dirty shoes, so choose colors that don't show the dirt—dark or multicolored rugs are good choices—and plan to toss them in the washing machine once a week.

QUESTION?

Are wood floors too much work to bother with?
Wood floors go with any style of decorating. They are a natural material that help make a room warm and comfortable. Wood holds up surprising well to wear and tear. Don't be afraid of wood floors—put scatter rugs down in the highest traffic areas, and enjoy the rest. Vacuum regularly so grit doesn't damage the floors, and wash them occasionally with warm water and a cleanser like Murphy's Oil Soap.

If the kitchen is the room that a commonly used entrance opens onto, a runner near the doorway as well as a handy carpet to hold dirty boots and shoes is helpful for maintenance.

If your kitchen floor is a hard surface like ceramic tile, you may want to consider even more extensive rugs since any glass or dish that drops on ceramic tile is likely to break.

▲ A throw rug placed in front of the sink will make standing in one spot while washing dishes, for example, a more comfortable task.

In the Bathroom

The bathroom floor begs for some throw rugs to step those clean bare feet onto or to keep feet warm while standing at the sink. If you are fortunate enough to have a large, luxurious bathroom, you can use the floor space for all sorts of great things. Chapter 13 outlines these in detail. Here we'll just mention that succulent plants love bathrooms for all their steam and moisture, so plan to load the bathroom up with some floor-sized plants if you have room.

The most important consideration in the bathroom is a flooring that holds up to water—not only for the protection of the flooring but also for safety's sake. Don't install a flooring in the bathroom just for its looks only to find out that it is very slippery when wet. Bathrooms get wet, plain and simple—the condensation from steamy showers and baths and even a trickle of water from the dripping condensation on the toilet tank can be dangerous on a slippery-when-wet floor.

In the Bedroom

The floor of your bedroom is likely to be the least decorative of all the floors in the house. This is a good floor space to keep clear of clutter for those dark late-night trips to the bathroom or the kitchen or the baby's room. If it is not carpeted wall to wall, a large carpet that encompasses the bed can provide warmth both for sleeping but also for stepping out of the bed onto a warm carpet. Throw rugs are not as necessary in a bedroom. The traffic in this room doesn't tend to be high since bedrooms are usually used by only one or two people. Putting down a throw rug tends to do little more than increase the chances that you'll have something to trip over in the middle of the night.

ALERT!

For inexpensive decorations, keep tabs on the markdown bins at your favorite home stores. Many stores have bins or shelves in some out-of-the-way place where they stash things like marked down items from the season just passed, odd lots, or things with slight blemishes. This is a great way to get quality accessories at prices that better fit your budget.

In the Living Room

With a wood floor and area carpets of varying styles, you can be consistent to almost any decorating style. A warm, dark, highly grained wood floor with a woven rug in natural tones of green and earth colors is perfect for the Arts & Crafts style. Put a black-and-white carpet with geometric patterns on a wood floor, and you get a great modern look. Switch to a rough pine floor and several rag rugs, and your room will be reminiscent of the colonial style.

Keep the living room floor more sedate to be a backdrop, so it does not overwhelm the decorating pieces of the rest of the room.

In the Dining Room

Stenciling on the dining room floor is a nice touch. When the time comes around to give those wood floors a buffing, consider adding a stencil border or corner details. See the sidebar for some specific tips.

The dining room that is mainly host to the dining table is a room where you can incorporate the flooring more fully into the decorating of the room. If the table is just one focal point and the room also has a sitting space, use area carpets to create separate parts in the room. You might put a warm, deep-pile rug under the full length of the table and chairs and lay a smaller rug as a centerpiece in the middle of a conversation area with upholstered chairs around the perimeter.

Stenciling is not exclusive to walls. Stenciling on wood floors before varnishing or on painted wood floors is quite traditional. Decorative border stencils or a rectangular stencil pattern resembling a small carpet are perfect decorative floor designs for any room in the house. Check any good hardware or department store, paint store, or the paint section of home improvement stores to find the paint, tools, stencil designs, and instructions you need.

Fitting Floors into Your Decorating Scheme

Perhaps the biggest decorating decision you need to make in regard to floors is color. Even wood creates a darker or lighter tone for the entire room. Carpeting, of course, offers a wide variety of color choices as well as patterns. Choosing linoleum almost always requires you to make color and pattern decisions. Painted floors can be light or dark, patterned or plain. As you can see, flooring definitely makes a huge impact on your decorating scheme.

If you have strong patterns and colors for your furnishings, a muted floor color will let those furnishings pop out. If your furnishings are plainer in color, pattern, and texture, perhaps they would liven up with a backdrop of a floor-sized carpet with a strong color and pattern.

Carpet will make a room seem warmer, so if it is an open room with a subflooring that is on the cool side, carpet might be the best choice. If the room is one in which you want to enhance a cool atmosphere, go for scatter rugs instead of a thick-pile wall-to-wall carpet.

In making good decorating choices, you should also consider the surface gloss of your flooring. High gloss shines and makes a room seem more spacious. Think of an expanse of ice where the glossy surface seems endless. Low-gloss matte finish creates a more subtle, intimate atmosphere.

If you are remodeling or building a new home, think about how the flooring will fit into your decorating plans. You don't have to decide every decorating detail ahead of time in order to choose flooring. If you can't decide on an overall style for your home or even a room, pick a classic flooring like wood or a neutral color carpeting since these can accommodate almost any decorating style you choose. And you can even change your mind without having to rethink the flooring!

A black-and-white check floor in the kitchen sets the tone for the decorating style of the kitchen. You simply can't ignore it. However, that doesn't mean it can only be the backdrop for one decorating style.

ALERT!

Staining wood floors a color is possible and can be an effective decorating tool, but be sure you choose a color you want to have around for a long time!

A checkerboard flooring is easy country style. A heavy wood table and wood chairs, decorative baskets, and crockery full of cut flowers all look great with a black-and-white floor.

It can also serve as the backdrop for a super modern look. A clear glass table can let the dramatic floor be seen through the expanse of the tabletop. Abstract art with bold splashes of color is very fitting with the black-and-white squares.

Stairwells

Stairwells are an area of the house often overlooked when it comes to decorating, especially if the stairwell is closed on both sides. Even though these areas may only be seen as you walk from one floor to the other, it is nice to have it be a pleasant walk!

Light up dark stairwells and staircases that have dark landings using spotlights or floodlights. You could even place a plant on a dark landing if you shine a grow light on it. Pick a plant that enjoys some shade anyway, and you'll achieve two goals at once: light up the landing, and at the same time decorate it with some live green foliage.

◀ This stairwell is lit by both an overhead light hanging from the ceiling and a window.

Stairwells can be great places to hang whimsical folk art or dramatic paintings. It's a nice surprise in such an out-of-the-way place. At the very least, paint the stairwell walls, carpet the steps (and vacuum them regularly), and make it a clean place that is a nice transition from one floor to the next. You can also install laminate flooring on stairs.

Stairwells that are open at least on one side offer a great wall to hang family pictures, collections of still-life paintings, miniature watercolors, or nicely framed postcards of the historic buildings in your town.

If the landing has enough space, add a shelf either at floor level or just above eye level and showcase a collection—beanie babies, porcelain dolls, model trains. A corner bookshelf could house those oversized art or architecture books, which are usually quite decorative themselves.

FACT

For historic and unique items to help with stair treads, check Yield House's Renovator's catalog—Renovator's Old Mill, Millers Falls, MA 01349; ✆(800) 659-2211; ✐www.rensup.com—for things like brass dust corners, carpet holders, and stair runner carpet rods.

Floors and Feng Shui

Feng shui doesn't have too much to say about floors. However, like all feng shui considerations, the floors in your home should be a material that is within your ability to maintain in order to keep your home as neat and orderly as possible. Flooring choices should be in keeping with the use of your home—if you have carpets, you will need to vacuum often. Linoleum and wood floors need to be swept and mopped regularly.

Throw rugs should be placed encouraging good traffic flow.

Stairwells are considered important energy transporters. For instance, avoid stairs that run straight toward the front door, as this allows good ch'i and financial opportunities to get away.

Chapter 9
Windows

Windows can be a significant decorative element in any room. Don't underestimate the role that windows play in your home decorating plans. A dramatic window or grouping of windows can be the focal point of a room, with all other decorating elements revolving around that point. But every window—dramatic or not—provides an opportunity to decorate and tie together the look of your home.

Practical Windows

From a practical standpoint, windows provide a home with important ventilation. You should always be aware of having strategic working windows to create cross-ventilation. Avoid decorating these windows in a way that obstructs them or makes them difficult to operate.

Windows also, of course, provide a room with natural light. In some rooms, such as a dining room or artist's studio, the more natural light the better. For other rooms, like the TV room or even the bedroom, the amount of natural light will either be kept to a minimum or at least be able to be easily controlled.

Windows are your view on the world. Clean windows provide a fresh view of the world outside, and keeping them clean should be considered a labor of love. Sparkling clean windows are a decorative element in themselves!

FACT

Natural Home Magazine showcases products and techniques to bring you closer to the earth and away from the plastic and chemicals of almost everything we buy today. Their Web site, *www.naturalhomemagazine.com*, reprints articles from current issues and has great links to earth-friendly products for your home.

Types of Glass

Although a decorating job is not likely to involve replacing windows on any grand scale, if you do have occasion to replace one or more (such as with a major remodeling job or adding on a new room), think very carefully through your selection of window style, number, and their placement. Typically, the more windows the better. You can always cover them with drapes or curtains, but you can't easily create windows where there are none.

With today's dazzling array of materials, the job of glass selection can keep you up at night before you ever get around to selecting trim color and window treatments. Double-paned, insulated, argon-filled, tinted: the possibilities are only limited by the imaginations of dozens of manufacturers.

First and foremost, pick something that is easy to clean. If a room will have a large expanse of windows, insulating factors may also top your list of priorities.

As you design your window layout, keep the overall style of your house in mind. That doesn't mean being locked into one specific style, but you also don't want to take your classic Georgian-style home and put countless blank panes of glass throughout. If your home's style is in keeping with multipaned glass, but the very idea of washing all those panes of glass sends you to bed with a migraine, get clear panes with removable mullion grids. Do they look authentic? No, but they still succeed in giving your house the basic look of one built before it was possible to make large sheets of glass, and the windows will be cleaner!

Different Rooms, Different Windows

The windows in your kitchen play a completely different role than the windows in your bedroom or in the bathroom. Consider their practical purpose when buying windows for different rooms.

The Bathroom

In the bathroom, windows can be mainly practical, providing a good light source for an often small, dark room. Bathroom windows also provide good ventilation. For this reason, the window or windows in the bathroom should be working windows, easily opened and closed. Decorative elements in the bathroom shouldn't get in the way of operating the window, and they shouldn't be things that fall off when a breeze blows through. Curtains should be able to push out of the way to let the air flow freely. And, of course, privacy should be a main consideration in window placement and window treatments in the bathroom.

The Kitchen

Unlike bathrooms, which are typically tucked out of the way, kitchens tend to be placed rather prominently in the home. This means that kitchen windows often look out onto a fantastic view. For people who don't like to cook or do dishes, the view from a great window seems to lessen the pain of these tasks they don't enjoy. For those who love to cook and be in the kitchen, a window with a great view just further enhances the experience.

▲ Large windows can really brighten up a kitchen. Here the top pane of each window is angled, making the windows themselves an interesting focus point of this room.

Depending on the style of house and where it is situated, kitchens often have more than one window. It's not uncommon to have a large window that does not have any sashes that open or close, plus one, two, or even more windows that work.

The Dining Room

Windows in a dining room often present less concern than almost any other room in the house. Unless your dining room windows look out onto a busy street and you prefer not to be "on view" while dining, window treatments in this room can be considered mostly for their decorative factor.

The more light in the dining room, usually, the better. At night, windows cleared of their window treatments can be great candlelight reflectors. Extensive window treatments can also be used to enhance the elegance of the room.

Window cleaning is essential to a polished home. Wash other parts of the window before the glass itself—dirt from frames, sills, and screens will dirty the glass. Wash windows on a cloudy day so the sun won't dry them so quickly and leave streaks. Use a no-lint cloth or sponge. Squeegee the window dry or rub with a dry no-lint cloth. And don't forget to wash the windows inside and out!

The Living Room

If your living room is also the TV room in your home, you will want to pick window treatments carefully. The first consideration is the incoming light in relation to the television screen. If your family doesn't tend to watch much television during daylight hours, this isn't as critical. But don't forget the kids, who may flop in front of the television to let down after school, or the armchair golfer who spends weekend afternoons glued to the tournament. Soap-opera lovers will want to watch their favorite shows glare-free. And during daylight savings time, even prime-time viewing can take place before dark. Be sure window treatments at least include shades that can be pulled up and down.

Bedrooms

Two main factors need to be considered when it comes to decorating the windows of a bedroom: light and privacy. What are the sleeping habits of the occupants of the different bedrooms in your home? Does someone work second shift and sleep in after daybreak? If the bedroom's occupant likes to rise at the crack of dawn, then curtains that can remain open may work just fine.

What kind of privacy do the window treatments need to provide? Is a simple roller blind enough? Does the room on the second floor look out over ten acres of forest or onto a busy street? The answers to these questions will influence the way the windows need to be covered.

Kids' Rooms

Windows can't be ignored in kids' rooms either. If the room is a playroom, a lot of good light is probably the key. Working windows to provide fresh air are great, and they are useful for ventilation if the kids spill milk or play with the dog—any playroom can use a good airing out once in a while!

Don't forget safety factors when it comes to kids' rooms. Do not use window treatments that have cords that kids could choke themselves with. And be careful of open windows that might let kids climb out and possibly injure themselves in a nasty fall. If the windows seem safely out of reach, consider the fact that kids love to climb. Furniture can make windows suddenly accessible. And if a child climbs up the draperies, will it all come tumbling down on them?

Several safety devices can be purchased for windows that kids have access to, such as window bars and childproof latches.

ALERT!

Making curtains is easy. The fabrics available make shopping for curtain material fun! But in order to ensure that your curtains hang the way they should, you need to cut and hem the fabric precisely to be sure it is straight.

Window Treatments

Although you can always create your own style of window treatments, there are some classic styles that you will run into as you make your choices.

Curtains or Drapes

Curtains are either gathered on a rod or attached to a rod by tabs, rings, or ties. Curtains don't necessarily open and close, but if they do, it's by hand. Draperies are the dressy style of window treatment. Traditionally they are attached to a traverse rod by hooks tucked into a band on the back of the drape and are intended to be opened and closed. They can be dressed up even more with undertreatments of sheer fabric, which also provides a minimal amount of privacy when the drapes are pulled open. The way drapes hang depends on the fabric and the amount of fabric used, as does the question of whether the drapes are lined or not.

Drapes also often have a heading, such as a valance or cornice. This can really emphasize the formality of your drapes and the whole room. Drapes can be very dramatic, with the drama enhanced according to the pattern and color of the fabric you choose.

Roman Shades

Roman shades are thick fabric window shades. Because of their thickness, they can't be rolled up. Instead, they are pulled up into folds with a cord that is attached to a series of rings. Roman shades are quite casual, but the fabric you choose for the side that shows in the room can make them appear a bit more formal; you can also dress them up with trim and borders.

They typically consist of a decorative fabric, a layer of batting like that used for quilts, and a liner that lays against the window. These three thicknesses are what makes them need to be folded not rolled, but it is also what makes them serve as great insulators on a drafty window.

The very nature of Roman shades makes them the kind of curtain you would tend to make yourself. If you do, pay very close attention to measurements and the prescribed widths and lengths since this will make or break the shade's ability to block out drafts.

Blinds

Many different kinds of blinds are at your disposal. Venetian blinds are the old standby from the second half of the twentieth century. They occasionally make a comeback and are perfect for a retro décor. Mini-blinds took their place and became all the rage later in the century. They are a little less clunky than the traditional wide-slatted Venetian blind, and they come in a dizzying array of colors, in vinyl as well as different kinds of wood.

Blinds also come in what are called "matchstick" style. These are roll-up blinds made of long, thin reeds or slender sticks that can be just the thing for a very natural decorating theme.

Basic recipe for window cleaner: 45 percent water, 45 percent rubbing alcohol, and 10 percent household ammonia. Mix up what you need in a spray bottle, and mark it "window cleaner." For safety purposes, it never hurts to mark the recipe on the bottle. That way, it's also right there when you need to make more.

All types of blinds can be a chore to keep clean. With the miniblind rage came a special dusting tool made of four or five fuzzy fingers that, when run horizontally, dusts several slats at a time. Nonetheless, if you aren't diligent in your blind dusting duties, these tools will do nothing more than spread the dust around and grind it into dirt.

Blinds are convenient, relatively inexpensive, and sometimes the perfect decorating choice. Alone, they are very modern looking. But combined with simple drapes or curtains, they can fit almost any décor except perhaps the most elaborate and formal.

Wood Shutters

Wood shutters are often used in country decorating schemes. Also called "plantation shutters," they come in some variations on a basic design, which is a wooden frame with a moveable rack of slats in the middle. Shutters are great for keeping the heat of the midday sun out while letting some air in if you open the slats. In the evening, they can be used the same way, only in this case the shutters would be swung closed for privacy while the slats still allow the air to circulate. They are often four panels wide, two on each side, and can be tall enough to cover the whole window. Shorter ones are installed on top and bottom.

Shutters can be made to fit in with any kind of informal décor. Simply paint them to suit the color scheme of the room.

Awnings

If you prefer bare windows but still need some protection from the sun, don't forget awnings. Many manufacturers, both custom and factory made, are offering stylish and fun designs and colors for awnings. Awnings can be retractable, but these tend to be expensive, so use them only where necessary. Overall, awnings can be an expensive choice. They give you a whole different set of considerations—now it's the design of the whole house's exterior you have to worry about, not just one room! Avoid bottom-of-the-line inexpensive awnings; they will look cheap and won't stand up to the weather.

Treating Windows to Color

Window treatments are one of the most prominent color-producers in any room. Along with upholstered furnishings and throw pillows, window treatments are where your choice of fabric creates just the right touch!

◀ A bold patterned curtain can make a great statement in a living room.

To create drama, surround your windows with fabrics that are bold in color and/or bold in design. The possibilities that exist these days are very exciting. If you want other elements of the room to create the drama, or you don't want drama at all, pick fabrics for window treatments that blend in with the color of the walls.

ALERT!

Window treatments do more than just cover the window. If you want to create a more dramatic look for a small window, hang drapes that are taller than the window from a rod above the top of the window frame. The same technique goes for if you want a window to seem wider—hang curtains that extend off either side of the window frame.

Perhaps you have an upholstered piece of furniture that is the centerpiece of the room. If the piece was custom upholstered at the time you bought it, you will be able to buy matching fabric and have drapes made. However, if the piece came as is you will have difficulty matching the fabric or color. Pick one color in the fabric and play off that for your window treatments. You need to decide whether you want the windows to take a backseat to the furniture and show off the upholstery with blander drapery color, or whether you want the draperies to work in conjunction with the furnishings to create a bolder overall look.

Texture and Fabric

Color is not the only important element in dressing your windows. Window treatments often mean wide expanses of fabric, and therefore texture becomes significant. The difference between the cool, crisp look of miniblinds and the deep, soft folds of a Roman shade is dramatic. Layered window treatments—for example, roller blinds with sheer drapes overhung with heavier drapes—create a different look altogether.

◀ Curtains don't have to be floor-length.

Texture also affects how the room receives light from the window. Obviously, more window covering means more subdued light. Leaving windows bare, with no treatments at all, can create a stark effect, but sometimes that look works perfectly in a room.

The fabric itself can make all the difference in your decorating style, whether the look is formal or country, modern or traditional.

Hardware Required

Drapes require track mechanisms to pull them open and closed. Rods can even become part of your decorating scheme, with ends that are vines or leaves or other designs. Curved windows don't even have to present insurmountable difficulty. You can purchase flexible or jointed rods to meet almost every oddity of window design. At worst, you may need a custom rod bent to fit, but for a prominent window, it's worth it.

If you like creative and whimsical touches, try some unusual hanging methods like clothespins or clothes hangers. Think creatively about other things as well—wood shutters don't have to offer just a country look. Painting them in bold colors or with some geometric decorations will give them a much more contemporary feel.

Do not frustrate yourself with cheap track rods for drapes. Buy the very best you can find. The mechanism should operate smoothly and glide freely back and forth. Also be sure to get one suitable to carry the weight of the fabric you choose.

Too Much of a Good Thing?

Windows allow sunlight into a room, which is typically a good thing! But there are some things that sunlight is not good for. Fabric and artwork can be adversely affected by sunlight, which can be responsible for both fading colors and damaging threads.

If you want the sun to shine into a room where it might do damage to your favorite print or your great-grandmother's antique quilt, be sure to carefully hang these treasures where sunlight cannot strike them.

It is best to hang these objects in rooms that have no natural light or where windows present a privacy issue and you usually keep the shades drawn anyway.

Chapter 10
Lighting

Lighting is an integral part of home decorating, with fixtures that can make or break your decorating job. It's a practical concern for the home decorator, too. After you've worked hard to decorate, you'll want your work to be seen! Don't consider lighting an afterthought; plan out a room's lighting scheme just as carefully as you would its furniture placement. Lighting goes hand in hand with every aspect of a room's décor.

How to Plan for Lighting

The first and most important thing to consider in a room is how the room will be used. You know that the kitchen is clearly a food preparation room, but does it also accommodate dining? Does it have space carved out for a desk and computer where the household budget is planned, finances evaluated, and bills paid? Does the dining room also serve up a reading nook? If you eat in front of the television, do you want a small dining area set up in the living room, or do TV tables (or your lap) take care of it?

You really can't overdo lighting—even if you have too many fixtures in a room, as long as they aren't huge and prominent or look like clutter, you can always keep them turned off. If you are doing a major renovation that will evolve into your next decorating project, make sure that ample electrical outlets are installed to accommodate any lighting scheme you decide upon once you start decorating. You can always leave outlets unused, hide them behind furniture or floor plants or pottery, or plug small nightlights into them that turn on only after dark or by a switch.

FACT

The American Lighting Association, a nonprofit organization, has a Web site that offers great information on energy tips and lighting considerations as well as a long list of links to Web sites of lighting manufacturers and retail stores. Check them out at *www.americanlightingassoc.com*.

Lighting Terms

Some basic terms used to talk about lighting are the following:

- *Fluorescent light*: Lighting that is produced by the excitation of fluorescent phosphorus by ultraviolet radiation.
- *Halogen light*: Lights that are produced by halogen gas heating up a metal wire to a high intensity.
- *Illuminance*: How much light falls on a surface. Measured in lumens per square foot.

- *Indirect lighting*: Lighting that reflects off a surface such as a wall or ceiling, with the rest of the light shining into the room.
- *Incandescent light*: A bulb that has a filament that produces light when it is heated to a certain point.
- *Reflector lamp:* A lamp that has a reflecting surface as a part of the lamp. Some lamps can have reflectors added to them.
- *Task lighting*: Lighting directed toward a specific location to illuminate a particular activity, such as reading or bill paying.

▲ Different types of lighting can be combined in one place to create cozy spaces. Included here are a lamp on the nightstand, a reading lamp attached to the wall, recessed lights in the ceiling, and a set of tall candles for mood lighting.

Illumination Range

When you choose lighting, you want to think about the range of illumination that a fixture casts. For instance, when selecting hanging fixtures, there are several factors to keep in mind, including the following:

- Choice of bulb.
- Height of light from the area or thing it will illuminate.
- Type and material of the shade.

You should decide how much of a room or area you intend to illuminate with a given fixture, and plan accordingly.

Fluorescent versus Incandescent

Fluorescent lights are the longer lasting and more efficient of the two main kinds of light bulbs. There was a time when the only fixtures available for fluorescent bulbs were shop lights or those recessed into dropped ceilings. These days, even floor lamps and table lamps can be bought with fluorescent or halogen bulbs that last several years (as opposed to the few months that incandescent bulbs last). They can offer warm light as well. In other words, you can now furnish your home with efficient lighting without making every room look like the workshop.

If you don't have a major lighting center near you, check with your local electric utility. Many are teaming up with innovative lighting manufacturers to offer interesting, affordable, and efficient fixtures.

Keep your lighting fixtures clean so they enhance your decorating work instead of detracting from it. Lamp heat attracts dust and insects, so lamps are especially prone to collecting dirt. Clean removable glass globes regularly using warm soapy water. Rinse with warm water. Towel them dry with a lint-free towel or air dry them. Dust off lampshades often to keep them from accumulating dust. If too much dust is allowed to collect, dusting will simply smudge it onto the lampshade.

Ambient Lighting

Ambient lighting refers to the overall illumination of a room. Natural light coming in through windows provides a certain amount of ambient light. If the room requires more, you will need to supplement the natural lighting. And, of course, at night when natural light is not available, the fixtures you install will take the place of the natural ambient light.

Every room should have some overall lighting, if for no other reason than to provide you with the means to see well when you are cleaning the room. However, there are many reasons to have ambient light in every room. You will be surprised how many times come up when it's important to be able to see in all parts of a room, whether it's as you move around redecorating, remodeling, cleaning, or just using the room.

Ambient light often takes the form of a central ceiling fixture. That fixture can be fluorescent, which provides a flow of light in the room. Many ceiling fixtures are covered with a glass globe. These are stylish and can be coordinated with other fixtures in the room, but they do not in themselves offer a large amount of light—the globe diffuses a lot of the light instead of spreading it into the room. In a room of any size at all, you will probably need more than one.

ALERT!

Glare from lights onto television and computer screens is not only annoying but is tiring to the eyes. Avoid glare when placing lamps and lighting fixtures in a room that is used for television viewing or computer work.

Fixtures that appear to be more like task lights can also offer ambient light if placed strategically. You can, for instance, direct track lights or recessed lights toward the wall so that they illuminate artwork and also so they bounce back off the wall, reflecting light into the room. Ceiling fixtures are available with four or five spotlights that can be directed toward each wall or corner of the room to wash the room in light from the center out.

Task Lighting

Once again, the key to selecting task lighting fixtures and placement is knowing how the room is used and deciding what areas of a room need to have light directed on them. Classic task lights in a living room are table lamps and floor lamps that direct light to a chair that is used for reading. If the living room is used for television viewing, a task light can also be used for ambient light if positioned in such a way that it doesn't glare off the television screen.

Task lighting is key in all rooms. Some important places to consider using task lights include the following:

- *The key areas in a kitchen where food is prepared.* Is there a light available at the counter near the range so the cook can see to cut up vegetables that go right from the cutting board to the pot on the stove?
- *Near the main telephone* to be able to clearly see the phone book, the keypad on the phone, and the message pad.
- *Foyers and halls.* Don't think just because no one spends time in a room like a foyer that it doesn't need good lighting. Any passageway like a hall needs at least some lighting to illuminate the path. If the foyer is the space that the main door opens into, you don't want guests to have to flounder around in the dark when they arrive.

Accent Lighting

Accent lighting is essentially light whose main purpose is to illuminate an object, rather than providing illumination for a task. Artwork is a perfect example of where accent lighting is used to make a painting or piece of sculpture stand out. Accent lighting is also used in other ways. For instance, you might use an accent fixture to reflect light off walls for mood and atmosphere but not necessarily for practical purposes. Accent lights can be used to illuminate a staircase or in an unused fireplace for that extra bit of light. Those lights that are reminiscent of patio parties are fun accent lighting—chili peppers, little horses, flowers—almost anything you can think of has been made into a string of lights.

Always have both ambient lighting and task lighting in every room. Even if you don't think you will ever use it, overhead lighting provides illumination for important chores like cleaning and rearranging furniture. You can always add and take away task lighting to suit the current uses of the room.

Types of Lights

There are many types of lights to consider, and choosing the right ones for your home's décor can be one of the most important and difficult tasks a home decorator faces. The right light makes all the difference. Buy the best quality you can afford—cheap lamps break quickly and get junky looking with shades permanently off-kilter and sockets falling out whenever you turn the lamp on or off.

Pendant Lights

Pendant lights are the kind that hang from the ceiling, usually with a chain or cord, and have a large lamp shade at the bottom. Don't be tricked into the conventional thinking that you can have only one pendant light in a room. If you need more than one, by all means go for it. Two over a dining table can be the perfect look—control the amount of light by making sure each pendant has a dimmer switch. Pendants can be wired in or can plug in. The plug-in style is obviously more appropriate for those that are hung near a wall, rather than the middle of a room, since you will need to find something to do with the cord, which you don't want draped all over the room.

Spotlights and Floodlights

Just as you do for out of doors, you can buy both spotlights and floodlights for your indoor environment as well. Spotlights illuminate a specific area and are used for task lighting. Floodlights bathe an area with light and provide great ambient and indirect lighting, creating a warm backdrop when directed to a wall. Spots and floods can be bought individually or in the form of track lighting. Use no more than three lights to a track to avoid an industrial look.

Sconces

Modified from their old-time candle counterparts, sconce lamps hug the wall and usually splash light upward or downward, not out.

Floor Lamps

Floor lamps are great for places where a self-standing lamp is useful, perhaps in a room where chairs are not against a wall. They don't take up space on an end table. Some of them even have built-in tables that encircle the lamppost.

FACT

There are dozens of suppliers of unique and period lighting. To find unusual lighting fixtures, check the advertisements in magazines that are devoted to your favorite decorating style. They will include Web sites and phone numbers. Some magazines are listed in Appendix A of this book.

Ceiling Fans

Ceiling fans are not strictly lighting, but almost all ceiling fans these days come with a built-in light fixture. Ceiling fans have become ubiquitous in the home, and they cost pennies to run—hardly anything when considered against their powerful ability to offset heating and cooling costs. Choose the highest quality ceiling fan you can afford—this fixture will get a lot of use, and you want it to be smooth and quiet, not wobbly with a grinding noise. The style range available today is considerable, from classic paddles to caned ones to highly contemporary styling with high-finish lighting.

Lights to Suit Your Decorating Style

Lamps can put the finishing touches on a decorating style. If you think you haven't quite achieved the Victorian look, try adding a heavy brass lamp with a velvet fringed lampshade and a couple of hurricane lamps with ornate globes. You'll find things looking up pretty quickly.

Colonial

The early colonists obviously didn't have electricity. But you can still be true to a Colonial look by taking advantage of the extensive availability of fixtures that mimic the candleholders of this era. Gaslight fixtures from later in early American life are also still available, either wired for electricity or still for use as gas lights. Electrified reproductions can be bought from many retailers who specialize in lamps.

Victorian

One needs to be careful to not go overboard when it comes to Victorian lighting. It is easy to get carried away! The heavily designed lamp fixtures of this opulent era are still widely available, both as antiques and as reproductions. Use them sparingly to decorate—not overwhelm—a room. Color is an important element of the Victorian-style lamps with ornate lampshades. These lampshades were often made in colors not discoverable in the rainbow.

A fun way to acquire lighting from this era is to rummage through tag sales and browse antique shops to find authentic Victorian style lighting for your decorating scheme.

Modern

A quick way to modern style when it comes to light fixtures is track lighting. Never out of style, these fixtures simply change a little to reflect current decorating trends. They are functional, bland, and they don't call attention to themselves, almost blending into their surroundings.

Arts & Crafts

The Arts & Crafts style engendered some gorgeous lighting fixtures. Rich woods mixed with leaded glass in striking designs evoking nature are classic hallmarks of the style. Frank Lloyd Wright, perhaps the most famous architect of this movement, was known to design even the light fixtures for a specific house. Many of these and other fine Arts & Crafts-style lamps have been reproduced.

Outdoor Lighting

Don't forget the outside of your home when it comes to lighting. At the very least, you want to make your home's walkways safe for evening guests. At the most, especially if you spend hours decorating your grounds with beautiful gardens, you don't want to let them go dark just because night falls.

Add accent lights to illuminate special trees, flowers, or planting. Get fountains with accent lights or even submersible lighting. If you are fortunate enough to have a gazebo or screen porch, make sure to light it up, both outside and in!

If running an electrical line is too expensive or too complicated, you still have options. Many outdoor lights now readily available operate on solar power, and battery-operated lights are always an option.

ALERT!

Electrical repairs and installation of electric fixtures are well within the reach of the ambitious do-it-yourselfer, as long as you keep a few precautions in mind. Unplug any appliance you are repairing. Shut off the power from any circuit that supplies any fixture or appliance you are working on that cannot be unplugged. Be certain to shut the power off from the circuit any time you are working with the line itself. Anything more substantial than a simple fix or single-fixture installation may well need a licensed professional who can follow legal building codes and keep your home safe.

Special Concerns in Kids' Rooms

Safety is the key word when it comes to lighting for kids' rooms. For the infant, this may mean simply not having a light or light cord within reach of the crib. However, the unique thing about designing lighting for kids is that the lighting needs for their rooms change approximately every two to three years.

After an infant is crawling, not only do the lamps need to be out of reach of the crib, but they now need to be out of the reach of a crawling child, one that might crawl out of its crib. Keep lamps up high and cords out of reach. If necessary, use only overhead lights that have been wired in.

One of the more versatile lighting fixtures is the accordion lamp. These lamps can be found in very stylish designs and come in either an accordion style or a style that lets them swing out on a bar. They put light exactly where it is needed. They push out of the way when you don't need them and are great for use in bathrooms, next to favorite reading chairs, or next to the bed. They also can provide nice ambient light when pushed back with the shade turned to face the wall.

As the child ages, safety remains an issue. Keep curious children from being able to examine the inner workings of a "live" lamp. Along with safety, the other thing that changes is the needs kids have for their rooms. Reading soon becomes important, then homework, then, yes, the inevitable need for electronic equipment, from computers to stereos to DVD players.

Until your child comes to the rebellious teen years, when the best color for a room is black and there is little need for lighting, have some fun brightening up the room with playful accent lighting, again well out of the child's reach.

Feng Shui and Lighting

It's not surprising that feng shui, with its strong focus on the natural elements, would place such strong emphasis on well-lit rooms. Good lighting is essential to good feng shui in your home; light enhances the energy flow and is always a good thing.

Natural light is always best. But when that is not possible, choosing appropriate lighting to illuminate any area is a must—conversation areas, dining areas, and work areas all benefit from appropriately bright (but not glaring) light. Crystals are good feng shui fixes for light that needs to be deflected.

There are lots of options for lighting, so show your home off in the best light possible!

Chapter 11
Furniture

Furniture is essential to the comfort and style of a home. Of course it serves practical needs first, but it also provides a decorative touch. With so many different styles and the variety of furniture pieces available today, you can create just about any look and feel you desire, without sacrificing usefulness.

A Brief History of American Furniture

When the British colonists began to settle the land that would become the United States of America, they brought some of their English and European-style furniture with them. It didn't take them long, however, to start creating their own. They took the styles they were accustomed to and adapted the furniture to fit the practicalities and changing social environment of their new home.

The early years of American history, sharply intertwined with British historical periods, left us with a few significant periods of furniture whose originals are highly prized collectibles and whose designs are still widely reproduced—for better or, in some cases, for worse. As you can imagine, in the years that followed the Declaration of Independence, furniture decorations became very patriotic, incorporating things like eagles and other strong, bold emblems.

As you choose your decorating style, being aware of these periods will help you select furniture suitable for your décor, especially if you live in a period house that was built in one of the great eras of American furniture. Sometimes you will simply love a piece for what it is. You may not care what period it hearkens back to, but it is still fun to know a bit about its history.

FACT

To review the most modern furniture styles, check out the Web site ✐ *www.retromodern.com*. Here you will find great examples of furniture of all kinds in molded plastic, glass, geometric shapes, and bold colors. It's a walk back in time, and if you are interested in decorating in a retro style, it's just what you are looking for.

Jacobean

The Jacobean era of furniture is, essentially, the entire seventeenth century, give or take a few years on either end. "Jacobean" is the Latin term for "of James," referring, of course, to King James I of England. Predominantly made of oak and ash, Jacobean furniture made use of strong, durable woods that were readily available throughout New

England. A lot of the techniques for constructing this furniture was based on early timber-framing techniques used in house building.

William and Mary

Yet another local interpretation of a British style, the William and Mary period ran from approximately 1690 to 1725. Some of the influences came from the Orient. The orientation of the furniture was more vertical, as opposed to the earlier Jacobean furniture which tended toward a more horizontal orientation. In these early times, Boston, Philadelphia, and New York were naturally, as the most accessible port cities, the furniture centers of the new colonies. This is the era when upholstered furniture really gained ground, relying on webbing and stuffing for strength and support. (Springs were not used until later in the eighteenth century.) This was the birth of the popular "wing chair," a high-backed chair with high arms that was said to be designed to keep away drafts.

Queen Anne Style

As with most other furniture styles both in the United States and in England, Queen Anne was named after the sitting royalty of the period. Queen Anne assumed the British throne in 1702, after the death of her sister, Mary, and William. This style in America is attributed to the period from 1725 to 1760. The colonists had settled and were beginning to prosper, allowing for the growth of a middle class. Furniture headed toward a style that was more delicate and refined. Although the American version of Queen Anne was considerably less elaborate than its European predecessors, this style became dominant in American furnishings.

Chippendale

Named for London cabinetmaker Thomas Chippendale, this style came about in the late eighteenth century, from 1760 to 1785. The prospering middle class was becoming wealthier. The Chippendale style was a combination of several lesser styles, including French and Rococo, both styles of decorating known for their inclusion of natural design elements like images of leaves, birds, fruits, and flowers. Again, like many adaptations of European furniture, the American counterpart was less elaborate but nonetheless was known for fancier elements, like the classic curved fronts on chests of drawers.

ALERT!

Don't get caught thinking that only pieces made by the original designers are considered valuable antiques. Authentic pieces in those designs that were made by cabinetmakers other than the original command huge prices at the antiques auctions as well. A recent issue of *Traditional Home* magazine reported a Chippendale chest made by an American artisan (circa 1792) sold for a whopping $4.7 million. Thomas Affleck of Philadelphia and John Townsend of Newport were master cabinetmakers who were known for their pieces made after the great British designer Chippendale's style.

The Federal Period

This was the era of George Hepplewhite, a London cabinetmaker whose name you will become familiar with if you chase after antique or reproduction furniture of the period from 1785 to 1810. This furniture style is marked by elegant simplicity and clear geometric forms. This was also the era of furniture maker Thomas Sheraton.

American Empire

This somewhat elaborately designed furniture of the period between the War of 1812 to about 1830 is said to be directly influenced by the French Empire style.

Shaker

The Shakers came to this country in 1744 in a classic escape from religious persecution. Theirs was a religion of strict tenets based on a principle of true simplicity. Simplicity was the name of the game in Shaker style of all kinds, including furniture. This style of furniture is very simple in form. It shows good workmanship and is designed to be, above all, useful.

Many craftspeople reproduce handcrafted Shaker-style furniture. A search online will reveal several fine outlets. Expect to pay top prices for this quality furniture that will become the antique of the future. The style can be found in many mass-produced lines as well, although the quality is definitely less fine than in the handcrafted pieces.

Although Shaker-style furniture is simple by design, it can fit well with many decorating styles since it does not stand out except by not standing out!

Beds

The classic piece that defines style from Colonial days is the four-poster bed. These can range from elegant, with turned or tapered posts sticking up from all four corners, to rustic and rugged. The sleigh bed gets its name from the fact that is resembles an old horse-drawn sleigh—the headboard and footboard are broad pieces of wood that curl outward at the top. The sleigh bed in itself ranges in style from elaborately turned to modestly turned, but whatever the style you choose, this bed is beautiful. It is also massive and will make a small room look cramped. Sleigh beds are available in metal as well as wood.

Canopy beds are perhaps the most elaborate bedframes of all. They give a room a romantic feel. However, like the sleigh bed, while a canopy can work in a small room, it will make it feel even smaller. If you want one even though your bedroom is not spacious, choose canopy fabric that is light in color and heft. That will help lessen the burden the piece makes on the room.

Dining Chairs

The chairs around your dining table should be comfortable, first and foremost. They don't have to exactly match your table, although most tables can be bought with matching chairs. Upholstered seats can add color and texture to a dining room. Windsor chairs are completely wood and, with their vertical rungs on the back, surprisingly comfortable. You can always add chair pads if you want, but be particular about how they are attached—they can tear unless they are delicately used. Shaker ladderback chairs combine simple wood styling with woven fabric seats that are remarkably comfortable.

◀ Chairs covered entirely in fabric or with slipcovers make a very elegant statement around a dining room table.

Upholstered Chairs

Overstuffed, wing chairs, slipper-back chairs—upholstered chairs, like sofas, can take on various forms. Again, first consider what you want out of a chair. Comfort? Style? Do you want wood legs that are exposed? How high do you want the arms? Should the arms be upholstered and part of the chair, or should they be raised wood with just the arm itself upholstered? Is the chair for a formal sitting area that will be used mostly by guests at a dinner party? Or is it for lounging in front of the television or for flopping beside a good lamp and reading a book?

These are all things you should think about when selecting upholstered chairs. Buy accordingly.

Sofas

Sofas are fun pieces of furniture to buy, but like beds, you need to shop especially carefully because this is an item that gets a lot of use.

Do you want exposed legs? Or a sofa that rests almost on the floor with short legs (known as "bun" legs, if the leg is a little ball that resembles a dinner roll)? Or a sofa with legs that has a "flounce" (sort of the bed dust ruffle equivalent for sofas) that hides the legs?

Another consideration is the level of formality the sofa has. Sofa backs can be straight, scrolled, curved (a full curve from end to end), or camel-backed (dipping down on either end and curving upward in the middle to a hump). The less fussy the back, the less formal the look of the sofa.

Cushion choice is also important. Do you prefer two cushions or three on the seat? Or do you perhaps prefer just one? The fewer cushions, the less dirt they collect. A single-cushioned sofa is not common. It is probably small, and the cushion is cumbersome to move to clean.

The "eight-way, hand-tied coil spring" is considered the hallmark of high quality when it comes to upholstered furniture. This support system consists of, as its name implies, coils that are hand tied by the furniture maker.

The arms of a sofa are another important consideration. What do you find comfortable? Try them out in the furniture store, and be sure to spend some time lounging on the floor model you are serious about. Do you prefer the arms to be the same height as the back, something you will find in the Chippendale style of sofas? Or do you like the arms dropped a few inches below the height of the back of the sofa? Wide arms in a sofa are a bit more casual, but they may be just the level of comfort you expect from a sofa. Don't go with wood arms in the sofa you plan to relax in, sitting in front of the television set, as this design element is much more formal.

Loveseats are popular, and they make a great second sofa in a living room large enough to hold both a traditional sofa and a love seat. It's easy to buy a matching love seat and sofa in many different styles and angle them perpendicular to each other to create a relaxing nook.

FACT

The process of "veneer" was used as far back as Egyptian times. Veneering is basically layering more expensive, high-quality wood on a less expensive, lower-quality wood base. But don't think just because something is "veneer" that it is necessarily less expensive. Sometimes the veneer is elaborate and quite costly. High-quality veneer pieces should last several lifetimes.

Sectionals have become increasingly popular as well. As a result, the sectional sofa is now available and in plenty more styles than just the huge velour-covered models. You can buy a sectional in high-quality leather or almost any other fabric. As an extra bonus, they are more versatile than ever, with additions like a recliner chair or even a recliner sofa!

Tables

The most significant table you will buy for your home is the dining room table. The next most important may be an informal table for eating in the kitchen. You can get tables in all kinds of materials, ranging from wood to glass.

How many people will the table need to seat regularly? This is going to be the determining factor for the size of the table, besides considering the room size of course.

Also consider whether you'll need to accommodate several extra people several times a year. If so, you will want a table that expands. There are options for expanding tables. A simple drop-leaf table, either rectangular or round, can change from a two-person table into a four-person table in seconds. If you need more expansion than that, many styles of rectangular tables allow for leaves, either by stretching the table out accordion style and setting leaves in the middle or by adding leaves to either end, known as "company boards."

Pedestal-style tables have one large leg coming down from the middle that fans out into four or five supporting feet. These are typically round, but pedestals also support small square tables as well.

For insider info in the furniture industry and the latest in fashions, check out ✍ *www.furnituretoday.com*. You'll learn more than you ever needed to know about the furniture business.

Guidelines for Buying Furniture

There are some basic things that as a furniture consumer you will want to keep in mind as you shop for the furniture for your home.

Buy the very best quality of furniture that you can afford. Both the frame and the upholstery or the exposed wood will hold up to everyday use. And when one of these elements finally wears out, it will be worth repairing.

Find a couple of furniture stores, and get to know them pretty well. The store personnel will come to know you and your tastes. They will be able to alert you to special sales and new products and lines coming in that they know you will like. Pick places with employees who don't mind if you spend time shopping around the store—but who also are attentive when you are ready for them. Shopping for furniture is a personal thing, especially if you are shopping as a couple. You will want to be able to talk things over both before and after you chat with a salesperson.

Don't just look at the surface of a piece, look underneath as well. This is where the real quality test will take place. On both the exposed and unexposed surfaces, look for neat, clean edges, flush joints, no glue hanging out—all these little blemishes signify lower-quality craftsmanship.

If a piece has drawers, make sure they glide in and out like silk, with no sticking, jamming, or getting caught up on anything. The drawers should sit square and not be off-kilter or show gaps around the edges.

FACT

Museums are great places to learn more about furniture styles and see the best examples of any given historical style. Some museums specialize more in furniture and home furnishings than others. The Whitney Museum in New York City is a great place to go see contemporary American style from the latter half of the twentieth century. For American history shown through the fine and decorative arts of approximately 1640 to 1860, visit the Winterthur Museum in Wilmington, Delaware. The museum was founded in 1951 and houses the incredible collection of Henry Francis du Pont.

Furniture Placement

There are two important things to do when deciding on furniture placement in a room. First, make a floor plan on graph paper, to scale if you can. Show doorways, both open ones and those with working doors, as well as windows and any other significant gaps in the wall, such as fireplaces or built-in bookcases. You can also use any of the many computer software packages available on the market for home decorating. Make a few copies of your basic floor plan, either printing them out from the computer or photocopying them. Start to play around placing furniture in the room. Begin with the pieces you have, and next consider pieces you would like to have. (This is a great way to start molding the dimensions you'll want when you begin to shop for a new piece.) Again, this plan works best if you've drawn the room and its contents to scale.

Second, move everything out of the room except the furniture that will take up floor space. If there are a lot of small pieces, move those out too, and concentrate on the larger pieces first. Plan to move the furniture at least two or three times to try out the most promising floor plans you designed on paper.

Most likely, there is a piece or two that can't be moved, shouldn't be moved, or will only be moved once to try something and once to its final resting place. Oftentimes these pieces of furniture will fit only in one or two places in the room anyway. Use your furniture to create a focal point in the room and work everything else around it—if the room is the dining room, concentrate on creating the dining space, then worry about chairs in a conversation area. Once you've chosen a floor plan, you can pull smaller pieces back into the room and arrange them, and then worry about all the accessories.

▲ Having a bed without a footboard can make it easier to make the bed each morning.

Outdoor Furniture

Don't forget to be picky when choosing your outdoor furniture as well. Teak and wrought iron are among the more common choices of materials for patio, garden, and deck furniture, but there are lots of other choices, such as painted wood. Although this furniture is designed to weather, you do want to be sure, just like the furniture in your house, that is it well constructed and won't fall apart after just a few seasons.

You can also decorate the outdoors with less substantial furniture and go for webbed, plastic, or cloth folding lawn chairs. The designs available are limited only by your imagination, and they can add great color to the yard. You can even use outdoor furniture inside in creative ways!

Chapter 12

Kitchens

The kitchen is one of the most used and useful rooms in your home. It is important that the kitchen be easy to maintain and clean and that the design promotes easy, efficient work. You can create a beautiful space that is both fun and practical by following just a few easy guidelines.

The Evolution of the Kitchen

The American kitchen has evolved since Colonial times into something that the 1700s cook would certainly not recognize. The pre Industrial-era kitchen was host to items such as pots, pans, wooden bowls, ironware, earthenware, butter churns, and other hand-operated paraphernalia that was required to keep the family's pantry stocked. To recreate this Colonial style in your kitchen, you need only search used and antique shops for mortar and pestle, pewter tankards, and candlesticks.

The Victorian era laid the groundwork for the kitchen gadget. Mass production allowed for the creation and manufacture of things like the meat grinder, sifting flour receptacles, and endless "can't-live-without" cleaning conveniences.

But the post-Victorian era is when changes really started to happen in the kitchen. By the 1930s, electricity was fast reaching every American household. Appliances like refrigerators took off in popularity, as did the precursors to almost all the conveniences that we now consider necessities.

FACT

Installing new kitchen cabinets is definitely more of a remodeling project than a redecorating project. However, if you find your cabinets too depressing to decorate around, and you want a significant change without the expense of new cabinets, consider having the existing cabinets refaced. This costs more than a few pennies (probably around $5,000 for the average kitchen), but that is still half of what it will cost to install completely new cabinets. If you like the general arrangement of the cabinets that are there, refacing can give you an inspiring, clean canvas to decorate around.

Bringing Style into Your Kitchen

Common kitchen styles range from country to retro diner to modern and anywhere in between. You may already have a basic theme. If your kitchen has the metal cabinets of the diner era, get yourself a Formica and stainless-steel table, some metal or heavy glass pendant lamps, and go with the flow. Items to accessorize this look are not difficult to find. Country-style kitchens are often predominantly wood—floors, cabinetry, and walls. The modern kitchen is very sleek and clean looking. If you can afford the latest in appliances, there are some fantastic choices out there!

▲ Appropriate task lighting is essential in kitchens. Lights hidden under cabinets provide lighting for reading recipes and chopping, dicing, and blending food. Lights that hang from the ceiling provide light to eat by (or cook by) above the island.

A Southwestern-style kitchen might reflect the natural colors of the Southwest region. Sand brown, sky blue, and natural tones with tile floors are all reminiscent of the natural environment that this style mirrors.

If you have young children living at home, consider an open decorating style very free of clutter, allowing room for play and the inevitable toys left in the kitchen. Accommodate your children in the kitchen, and you can cook while keeping an eye on them at play. This method also means you can spend time interacting with your kids while you create dinner.

If your kitchen came equipped with metal-style cabinets, you don't have to suffer with whatever color they are. If you want to keep them but you also want a change, dismantle them and check with a local auto body shop to see if they will do a paint job on them.

Clean Color Schemes

Color in the kitchen is important. White is certainly a common choice. It is the color we associate with cleanliness, and clean and the kitchen go hand in hand. However, dirt shows up very easily on white, so you'll need to be very studious in your cleaning.

Black makes a very modern kitchen, and it also can appear very clean. Most appliances now come in black, and black is a very good background to show other colors against.

Either white or black as the predominating color offer endless opportunities to accessorize with other colors. Yellow and green are cheerful colors for a kitchen and are great accents with either black or white. Red is always a nice color accent, but use it sparingly if you follow feng shui practices, as outlined at the end of this chapter.

FACT

A valence is a horizontal curtain that runs the full width of the top of a window and is only a few inches long. They are easy to make. Seam both sides, the bottom, and the top. Then fold the top over to make a casing for the curtain rod, and *voilà!* you have a valence. You can use the very best fabric since you need barely a half yard per valence; if your window is wider than the standard width of most fabric (44 or 60 inches), make two or three valences. Pick fabric patterns that are easy to make even—either bold flowers or large patterns with vegetables and herbs, or use calicoes or striped fabrics that offer natural cutting lines.

Window Designs

Traditionally, a window over the sink is almost a given. In old homes that were built before technology allowed for large panes of glass, all windows were multipaned. Such glazing in the kitchen is very appealing, but keep in mind that these small panes are a little more of a cleaning project under even the best of circumstances. Cleaning becomes even more of a chore in the kitchen, where grease and splatters are common.

It's important to have windows that open, if at all possible. You also may want to avoid curtains for the same reasons of dirt and grime; valences in great fabrics are lovely accents and leave most of the window for viewing. Kitchens don't usually have the same privacy issues as bedrooms and bathrooms, so let the light in!

ESSENTIAL

Don't forget a place in your kitchen for cookbooks. These can become decorative items themselves if you give them their own place of prominence in your kitchen. Carve out a nook to create sturdy bookshelves or scatter them in smaller numbers in various spots throughout the kitchen.

Fuss-Free Walls

The ability to clean is of utmost importance when considering the wall covering for a kitchen. Especially around the stove, choose materials that can be wiped and even scrubbed. If you want to use a fussier material in most of the kitchen, surround the stove with formica, paneling, stainless steel, or at least high-gloss paint.

Painted walls are always prime candidates for the incredible array of wallpaper borders now available. They can bring a fun element to the kitchen with little expense. They are easy to install and can be wiped clean, just like any other wallpaper.

You likely have hanging cabinets and floor cabinets, and these probably make up the majority of your kitchen's wall surface. Between the wall cabinets and the countertops, you can choose to hang things like a paper-towel holder, a knife holder, and even under-the-counter appliances like can openers and coffeemakers. All of these things also, of course, come in countertop models.

Choose what works for your space—do you have a lot of counter space? Then countertop accessories are not a problem. But if your counter space is limited, don't clutter up the kitchen with a countertop paper-towel holder. A simple one that attaches under the cabinet will save some counter space for the real work of the kitchen.

Common decorations for upper walls in kitchens that have wall space not covered by cabinets are old-fashioned Jell-O molds or decorative plates, with all kinds of possibilities for hanging hardware. You should wash these decorative items once every few months.

Ceramic Tile

Ceramic tile in the kitchen can add a nice dimension to the room. But you don't have to go to the time and expense to do an entire wall or floor to incorporate the great look of ceramic tile. Consider doing just a three-by-five-foot section on the floor at the door. Another great place for tile decoration that's also useful is the area behind the sink (known as the backsplash). You could even run one row of tile along the countertop behind the sink.

ESSENTIAL

You can find ceramic tile to reflect any decorating style. There are painted tiles showing country scenes or farm animals; you can create simple geometric patterns with black and white tiles for a modern look; or, if you shop in ceramic tile stores, you can even find tiles with raised patterns that make very interesting and unique touches.

To install ceramic tile, follow these steps:

1. Apply a layer of tile adhesive to the area.
2. Press the tiles into position, using spacers at each corner to leave a narrow gap between each tile. (Some tiles come with built-in spacers

entryway

kitchen

Elizabeth Whiting & Associates/Dennis Stone

Elizabeth Whiting & Associates/Neil Davis

bathroom

Elizabeth Whiting & Associates/Andreas von Einsiedel

Elizabeth Whiting & Associates/Steve Hawkins

dining
room

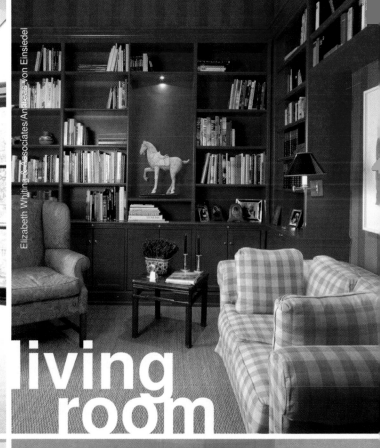

living room

kids'
room

master bedroom

patio

or, as with most premade mosaics of small tiles, may come held together already spaced on a webbed backing.)

3. Let the adhesive dry for a day or so, then fill the seams between tiles with grout. Grout comes either premixed or in powder that you mix with water. (You can also purchase colored grout or coloring you can add to grout powder, as well as waterproof grout.) Work the grout into the seams, pressing it with a damp, dense sponge, which can also be used to wipe away the excess that will end up on the tile surfaces.

4. To really achieve a professional look, use a tool that will give the seams a finished, uniform surface.

Floors That Work

The basic floor surface of your kitchen will dictate the appropriate accessorizing you may want to do with scatter rugs. If the floor in front of your sink or stove is a hard surface, a comfortable rug is a must for the time spent standing at the sink washing dishes or in front of the stove cooking. If you are planning a major kitchen remodel, and it includes replacing the flooring, consider installing permanent comfortable flooring in the areas in front of those heavily used places. The chances are slim that either the sink or probably even the stove will move anytime soon, so you can cut a throw-rug size space out of your linoleum or wood floor and piece in a few squares of cushioned square tile or even a piece of carpet.

ALERT!

In your attempt to make your kitchen efficient, be mindful at the same time of what you are placing low enough to be in the reach of small children. For instance, built-in knife racks at kid-level are just not a good idea under any circumstances. Even spice jars that could contain dried cayenne pepper would be harmful if a child got the hot pepper in his or her eyes.

Carpeting overall in the kitchen is not unheard of, but it isn't the most practical choice. Despite your best efforts, crumbs and food are going to end up on the floor during food preparation or even just as you're getting something out of the refrigerator. This food will inevitably get ground into the carpet, making it just a little more difficult to keep a clean kitchen.

Lighting for Cooking

The kitchen is a key room in which to create both task and ambient lighting. During meal preparation, the cook tends to be wandering all over the kitchen, both within the work triangle (the space between the stove, sink, and refrigerator) and out. The room should have some overall lighting as well as task lighting close to each of the work areas.

Pick unobtrusive light fixtures if you need to add self-standing lights (opposed to recessed or wired ceiling fixtures). Wall or hanging pendant lamps leave the counters free for utensils, small appliances, and decorating items that the kitchen counter tends to need to accommodate.

There was a time when ranges came automatically with a built-in stovetop light. Since the proliferation of the microwave range hood, which provides an overhead light for the stovetop, ranges often don't come with a light. This is something you will want to provide if you don't plan to install a microwave range hood. The important thing is to have plenty of lighting in all the right places to showcase your color choices, the kitchen's décor, and of course to light up those many areas where you will be performing tasks like cutting and chopping or reading recipes.

If you don't like the clutter of countertop appliances, consider installing an "appliance garage." More a garage door than actual garage, this is a flap that comes down from the bottom of the cabinet to the counter. It can match your cabinets or countertop and hides the small appliances in their own space, keeping them free of dust yet easily accessible. This is important since they are probably items you use almost every day, like your coffeemaker or toaster. Be careful to cool these hot appliances down, however, before you close the garage door!

Kitchen Furnishings

For an eat-in kitchen, the most important furnishing consideration is the table. If the kitchen table is the only place you and your family eat, the table should be appropriately sized. If you need to squeeze a table into a kitchen that really doesn't easily accommodate the size of table that you need, look for tables that have folding leaves. You can also use a table that spreads out with middle leaves that you can remove whenever you need to. Keep in mind that it takes a little more effort to expand the table this way than with the drop-leaf method, which may become a hassle if you need to do it everyday. The other difficult consideration with removable leaves or "company boards" (that expand the table on either end instead of in the middle) is that you'll have to find a place to store them.

▲ Having barstools or chairs around a peninsula in the kitchen is a great way to create a casual dining area in the kitchen.

Finding a table to meet your decorating scheme shouldn't be difficult. We've already mentioned the diner-style stainless steel table.

Tables that suit a country décor abound. Almost always made of wood, a country-style table typically has a heavy look that is especially suited for casual kitchen dining.

After the table, the next most important furnishing to consider is chairs. The chairs for a kitchen dining arrangement should be casual and relaxing, like the table. Rustic Windsor style chairs, matching chairs for the 1950s diner style, and comfortable modern wood chairs with cushions all make for great kitchen dining décor.

Perhaps your kitchen has a counter that begs for stools. You can get stools to match just about any chairs. Place a couple at the counter for extra casual dining or for a place where you can sit and have coffee as you read the paper each morning.

Other kitchen furniture may include a hutch, which is great for dish storage in kitchens lacking lots of cabinets. Kitchen islands were once the rage, but now it seems more convenient to have a moveable kitchen island. This usually takes the form of a rolling cutting block that also offers some additional storage—drawers, shelves, or a pegboard to hang things. Sometimes people think they need extra large kitchens to include these kinds of things, which is what makes easily moveable furniture great for small kitchens. This furniture can be pulled out when needed and pushed aside, out of the way, when they aren't. A kitchen island on wheels can be quickly transformed into a kitchen peninsula when it is rolled off alongside the wall.

Don't add a lot of nonkitchen stuff to decorate your kitchen. Cookware, utensils, and much of what you will actually use in your kitchen make perfect decorative items if you pick quality and stylized things. What could be cooler that a forest green KitchenAid mixer?

Practical Accessories

Choosing accessories for the kitchen may be the most fun you have decorating! Kitchen or kitchen and bath stores have expanded into outlets for much more than just pots and pans. Even picking out a knife holder can be a multitrip shopping experience.

Practical accessories for the kitchen include the little things that keep everything you need in convenient places. Canister sets can be so stylized that they almost become the centerpiece of your kitchen decorating style. You can choose from country sets of rustic crockery, contempo sets of highly lacquered ceramics or bright glass in colors like red and cobalt blue, or diner style in sleek stainless steel.

Dishware makes a logical choice of decorative items for the kitchen. New cabinet door handles and drawer pulls also make a fun, simple, and inexpensive way to perk up the kitchen and with great impact. Just remember that you may have to fill old screw holes and repaint if you change them.

The Feng Shui of the Kitchen

The Chinese word for wealth is quite similar to the Chinese word for food. Therefore, the room where food is stored and prepared naturally holds a high place in feng shui consideration. Here are a few feng shui principles for kitchen design:

- Your stove should be situated so that the user's back is not to the entrance of the kitchen.
- Keep the stove, especially the burners, very clean. The stove is the most auspicious of appliances because it generates heat and cooks food, both wealth symbols.
- Use all the stove burners regularly, and not just the same one or two over and over. Your business prospects will be good if you keep heat and energy passing through all these openings.
- Place a mirror over your stove if possible. If four burners are good fortune, eight are better.
- White is a good color for a kitchen. It is the color of purity and cleanliness, both good traits for a kitchen. And white is the color of metal, which is a good companion to the kitchen's predominant element of fire. For that reason, a red kitchen would be disastrous!

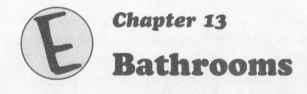

Chapter 13

Bathrooms

Don't forget the bathroom when it comes to decorating. There are many options for bathroom décor. Keep things simple and easy to maintain so that the bathroom can be adequately clean and well functioning. You can have attractive bathrooms that are as stylish as the rest of your home.

Styling the Bathroom

You will probably want to decorate the main bathroom in keeping with the style of the rest of your house. In houses with more than one bathroom, there may be a combination of a main first-floor bathroom, a small first-floor "water closet" sized bathroom, and a master bathroom off the master bedroom.

The decorating choice for the master bedroom's bath is simple—decorate it in the same style as the bedroom. The other bathrooms are up for grabs. You don't have to have a specific decorating style for bathrooms. Simple, efficient, and easy-to-clean are the key elements. Any style you choose will be dictated by your choice of fixtures, such as toilet, bidet, sink, vanity, tub, and shower stall. The style of these can be the overriding factor in your bathroom décor.

Achieving a Specific Look

An Art Deco bathroom might include some geometric shapes in the classic color combinations of the early part of the twentieth century; black and a muted natural tone like sky blue or a lively green would be perfect with stark white fixtures and chrome accessories.

Cleaning is a top priority for bathrooms. Decorate simply and in a way that keeps cleaning easy and therefore likely.

Victorian-style bathroom decorating can be fun, but don't get carried away with much clutter and fuss in the bathroom. Heavily flowered wallpapers and fabrics, ornate mirrors, and elaborate shower curtains can keep you in the style without being cluttered. If you want Victorian knickknacks in this heavily used room, consider hanging a lovely glass-fronted curio shelf on the wall to help keep a knickknack collection from becoming a dust collection.

Off-the-Wall Ideas

The bathroom is a great place to go a little wild. It is such a private room that you can really surprise guests with a creative bathroom, and you can brighten up your own routine by walking into a fanciful bathroom. Some ideas include the following:

- Use a dramatic flooring and help it stand out by surrounding it with more muted décor.
- If you are making huge changes in the bathroom that include plumbing needs, consider allowing your plumbing to be visible. Copper piping common in household plumbing can be very attractive. The added bonus is that exposed plumbing is easier to fix because it keeps you from tearing out walls to get to it.
- To have some decorating fun in the bath without going to huge extremes, consider a colored toilet—black or red—instead of the typical white or "bone" colors.

These simple ideas can dress a bathroom up and allow you to decorate around some fun fixtures.

Color Considerations

Victorian style lends itself to dark and enveloping colors. Because bathrooms involve the use of a lot of water and often have a steamy atmosphere, dark colors can create a foreboding feeling. Light colors help make the bathroom seem clean and airy, especially if the room is in the center of the house with no outside windows that can be opened.

Modern-style fixtures, such as sleek glass shower enclosures and expansive whirlpool tubs, are well accompanied by black accessories and steel or chrome metal faucets. Splashes of color are always nice in any room. Don't forget to brighten up the bathroom with touches of red, green, purple, or yellow. Any color in small bits is appropriate anywhere in the house, including the bathroom!

Windows and Lighting

Functioning windows, if at all possible, are simply a must in the bathroom. There is nothing better than being able to open windows and air the room out. If you don't have windows in a bathroom, definitely make sure to have a ventilation system. They are easier to install than you might think.

◀ Thick glass tiles make a great privacy wall in a bathroom.

Keep window treatments in the bathroom simple. You will need to take privacy into consideration, but you don't want the bathroom curtains to be so prominent that they become clutter.

Bathroom lighting doesn't need to be extensive, but what is there is very important. It is best to have a light switch at the entrance to the bathroom to make the room well lit before entering. This is because many home accidents happen in the bathroom. You want to be able to see where you are going and not trip over things, especially if members of the family or houseguests are prone to making trips to the bathroom in the middle of the night. A nightlight that comes on automatically at dusk or a small lamp that you leave on at night is helpful. A lamp can help add to your decorating scheme. Don't let yourself be trapped by ideas of what is "typical" for bathrooms; any lamp will work.

The area around the sink, where hair care, shaving, tooth care, and other detailed health and beauty care takes place, needs to be well lit with flattering light in a range of intensities. If you have closet space in the bathroom, install a light that comes on when the door opens or one of those battery-operated "press" lights.

ALERT!

A main concern for bathroom lighting above or beside a mirror is that it not create shadows. A light bar is great for this area, but be sure it runs the full width of the mirror.

What Covers the Walls

As in the kitchen, you will want to make sure the walls in the bathroom are easy to clean. Use gloss paint, paneling, vinyl wallpapers, or ceramic tile—anything that is easily washed. Paint is easily freshened up and makes a great choice for bathroom walls.

Don't consider the bathroom exempt from art. Framed photos, prints, and fiber-art pieces are great in the bathroom. However, don't hang any valuable one-of-a-kind originals in a room that is so prone to an overdose of steam and the accompanying potential dangers of mold and mildew.

You can't have too many mirrors in the bathroom. Mirrors make small rooms appear larger, and they are always important if the bathroom is where you put on makeup, dry your hair, shave, or even change your clothes. Don't forget to provide good lighting next to and around mirrors.

Although the big home improvement warehouses have a good range of selection in the bathroom fixtures department, you may want to include plumbing stores and, if you have an older home, salvage yards in your search. Besides fixtures, don't limit your search for accessories only to bathroom-specific stores. Use your imagination, and look everywhere.

Floors for Getting Wet

The main flooring for the bathrooms in your home could be any of the typical flooring materials, such as wood, linoleum, ceramic tile, or even carpet. For any of the hard floorings—almost anything except carpet—you will want to consider safety factors.

Wood and linoleum can be slippery when wet, some more than others. The easy way to offset this is with bathroom throw rugs. Scatter rugs designed specifically for the bathroom have rubber backings that stick well to almost any floor surface and don't soak through from above when wet feet step on them.

Coordination is easy. Bathroom accessories are big business, and you can get sets that include towels of all sizes, scatter rugs of several sizes and styles, toilet tank and lid covers, tub liners, shower curtains, and even soap dishes and toothbrush holders that match in color and pattern. There is no need to forsake style for safety.

FACT

There are some truly extraordinary and unique bathroom items available for the discerning decorator with an extensive budget. Sink and bath faucets can be had for literally thousands of dollars. You don't need to be in the airport to enjoy the no-touch faucets that come on automatically when you stand in front of them; if ultramodern is your decorating style, these sensorized faucets are available to homeowners as well. Bathtubs can look like works of art (and be just as expensive as a fine artwork). For example, a reproduction copper tub from Kallista (at ℡ (888) 452-5547) will run you over $40,000—at least that price tag includes the faucets!

Furnishing Options

The furnishings required in your bathroom will greatly depend on the size of the room and the amount of use this particular bathroom gets. If the bathroom is large with the atmosphere of a nice spa, and if it is used for pedicures, manicures, and other beauty treatments, make room for a comfortable chair placed near the vanity or, if the bathroom is big enough, with a small table next to it where you can place necessary items.

As you plan your bathroom's furnishing and accessory needs, be sure you keep in mind the question of how much closet space your bathroom will require. Make sure there is storage space for towels. If no linen closet exists, get creative. Look for interesting racks, tables, or shelving that may also provide other uses as well. Maybe the bathroom is big enough to fit a dresser—these major pieces of furniture can be chosen to fit in with or actually establish the decorating style in the bathroom. A simple painted small dresser with sleek handles creates quite a different look from an ornate Victorian-style vanity with a large scrolled mirror. Don't get caught up with the usual furniture. If you have the room, look for interesting pieces to solve your needs.

Tubs

The most important furnishings in the bathroom are, of course, the working fixtures themselves. If you have an old, stained bathtub that is looking unpleasant for bathing, consider the recently popular method of a one-piece insert that drops over everything—walls and tub. It can make a bathroom look like new in just a day. They can be expensive, so it's not something you'll want to do if you are planning a major renovation within three years or so. But if it's likely to be ten more years before you'll be ready to strip the old tub out and do something totally new with the area, a tub insert is a good way to go.

Toilets

Although it may be a little beyond decorating and more in the realm of remodeling, toilets are not that difficult to replace. This change is a good thing to do to achieve new water efficiencies. Toilets have come a long way over the years. Besides being available in period-imitating Victorian style with overhead tank and wood lids, even the porcelain standbys offer style and comfort and are available in a range of colors like never before.

Sinks

The classic wash basin in the bathroom is the sunken bowl with mixing faucets. The sink is one place where you can make a strong style statement and create a focal point without much effort. A current trend in wash basins are those that sit on the countertop. Handpainted basins make a dramatic addition, and the drama of either of these basin styles can be enhanced with unique faucets. Pedestal sinks give a more open appearance to a small bathroom, but good looks come at a price, since the open appearance also eliminates any potential storage space that a typical vanity would provide.

Don't forsake safety for decorating style when it comes to bathrooms. Use appropriate rugs and tub liners that make it less likely to slip in this room that is often wet and often the site of serious home accidents.

Faucets

Faucets often are treated as an afterthought. But the wide array of products that are readily available makes it possible and even easy to give your bathroom a whole new look just by replacing your faucets. An arched faucet in either the sink or the tub quickly creates an elegant effect in any bathroom. Combine materials such as porcelain and chrome to create more interesting décor.

Fixture Materials

Bathroom fixtures can dictate a bathroom style. Several materials are available to choose from and they all create a distinctly different look. Here are a few examples:

- *Brass:* The deep, rich gold tone of brass works well with a Victorian decorating style. Brass is warm and a good choice with a backdrop of dark walls and carpeting, such as a deep red.

- *Chrome:* Chrome in the bathroom is among the most common choices. It offers a similar effect as the other silver-toned materials such as stainless steel, nickel, or pewter, but has a distinct high gloss.
- *Pewter:* The muted look of pewter can really tone down an overall look. Pewter can be quite classy mixed with gold or even porcelain.
- *Nickel:* Nickel (usually nickel-plated brass) is the silver-toned material that is in between the high shine of chrome and the more muted look of pewter.

Accessories

The bathroom is often jokingly referred to as "the library." It is certainly a place where most everyone has spent time reading. A magazine rack that is restocked regularly with fresh magazines is an appropriate accessory for just about any bathroom.

The common accessories you will want to include in any bathroom are toilet tissue holder, soap dish, toothbrush rack, and a mirror. If the bathroom is a main one used for shaving and hair care, make sure the mirror is prominent and over the sink—you shouldn't have to lean from the sink to the mirror to shave every day.

FACT

When bathrooms are shared by more than one person, consider two sinks when space is available. If it's possible to create some privacy around these sinks, that's even better. And to add just one more his-and-hers luxury, install two showerheads at different heights.

Other accessories that help keep the bathroom neat and clean are organizing items like a hair-dryer rack or stacking containers for beauty and health care supplies that are used often but perhaps not every single day.

Plants are great accessories for the bathroom, especially primary and master bathrooms where plants can get moisture from the steam from daily showers and baths. And they are cheery, too.

One bathroom accessory that can be a whole lot of fun is the shower curtain. Shower curtains come in a wild array of patterns and styles, from cute farm scenes, kids' favorite cartoon characters, fishbowls, floral patterns, solid colors, and anything else you can imagine—including many you probably hadn't imagined! They are expansive by nature and a necessary item in most bathrooms. They're also relatively cheap and can be changed often to keep them fresh and fun.

If you have a glass shower enclosure, everyone will need to work to keep it from clouding up with soap scum. This requires constant diligence and cleaning after every shower. They are not as fun to decorate as tubs that need shower curtains, and they can't be simply and cheaply replaced every time they look too dirty. But they do offer a bathroom a neat and modern look.

QUESTION?

What is the history of the modernized bathroom?
Indoor bathrooms—as opposed to separate outhouses—became the norm in American homes in the first half of the twentieth century. Bathrooms were quite elaborate then, perhaps out of nostalgia for the decorating style of the Victorian era, which is when indoor plumbing was created. In houses with the space, bathrooms were large, with furniture and substantial bathtubs.

Baths for Two

In a household with two adults and one or more children, having more than one bathroom is almost as much a necessity as having any bathroom at all. If your house has a master bathroom, and you find that your kids take occupancy of the second bathroom during the key hour when everyone is getting ready for work or school, one thing that might help alleviate congestion in the bathrooms is installing two sinks in the master bathroom. You and your spouse can get ready at the same time. The added bonus is that you can personalize your own sink space and, with some creative thinking, make it somewhat private as well.

The two sinks can be placed side by side or facing each other, if space allows. If you don't want to install a permanent wall between the two, buy matching mirrors and hang them back-to-back to separate the space.

▲ Having two sinks means not having to fight for space when two people's morning schedules coincide.

Be sure to light each sink and mirror well for makeup application and shaving. To conserve countertop space, consider vanities with built-in drawers for storage of personal items. Many of the items used in closet storage systems could prove useful for storage in tight bathroom space as well. Another option is to buy clear plastic storage containers where you can keep similar items in one place. You can lift these systems out of the vanity closet to have on the countertop only when you are using them.

Feng Shui in the Bath

Bathrooms are not to be ignored when it comes to feng shui considerations. First, consider how easy it is to maintain and keep up a clean bathroom. Good feng shui in a household is considered to be very much enhanced by the smooth running and cleanliness of the bathroom.

Keep your toilet lids shut. Water is equated with wealth, and you don't want your fortune to easily be able to go down the drain!

Try painting your bathroom green. This relaxing color is considered conducive to good digestion and health. Blue is also a good color choice, since it is the color of water and will help keep the plumbing in good working order.

The position of the bathroom relative to the rest of your home is, as you might expect, also important. Bathrooms are private places that are best tucked off to the side away from kitchens and other rooms where people gather. You probably won't be able to easily move your bathroom's location—a major change like that is well beyond the scope of decorating anyway—but you can use common feng shui fixes such as mirrors and wind chimes to deflect the room's energy away from the central gathering spots. Also, it is best if the bathroom is not visible from the entrance to your home. If you can't avoid this, keep the bathroom door closed always. (E)

Chapter 14
Dining Rooms

Is your dining room reserved only for special occasions? Perhaps you also use it as a place where you can spread out some take-home work, where you or the kids do some studying, or maybe there is an area in one corner for relaxing and reading. Even so, the room's most prominent piece is probably a dining table surrounded by chairs. But don't just stick in a table and a few chairs; instead, have some fun decorating this room!

Dining in Style

The dining room is a prime canvas for all of the classic decorating styles. The dining room and living room are often in close proximity, usually linked by a hallway or even open to each other, so you will want to consider their style collectively. Perhaps they simply give a nod to each other without completely meshing with each other stylistically. However, you can also have fun with that and pick up on a color or a theme from one room to the other.

Dining rooms are a great place to showcase collections. If you host dinner parties, your collections are sure to be enjoyed by guests. And if your dining room is used solely for dining, there is often enough room for furniture that can be used for displays.

You can achieve a country style in the dining room pretty quickly with the following pieces:

- A round oak table with a chunky pedestal for rustic country or a cherry table with tapered legs for a more delicate country look.
- An open hutch with pottery, crockery, baskets, and mugs.
- Informal curtains or wooden shutters, braided rugs on the floor, and artwork of farm scenes, animals, and landscapes.
- Pitchers filled with cut flowers or wildflowers, houseplants, and herbs.

ESSENTIAL

Botanical prints make great wall art for the dining room. Frame three or four of them alike and group them to make an impact.

Or for a look back, try these familiar themes:

- *Sixties:* Bold colors in devil-may-care combinations, low ambient lighting, and unframed flat mirrors—as well as perhaps just one lava lamp—will get you started.
- *Diner:* Although diner styling is probably more suited to the kitchen, you can carry the theme to the dining room using chrome and plastic furnishings, clocks boasting advertisements for food, and the appropriate sugar bowl, salt and pepper shakers, napkin holder, and

condiment bottles for accessories for the table.

- *Arts & Crafts:* Again, the table and chairs will set the tone for this style. Add a Craftsman-style bookcase, a couple of Stickley chairs in a conversation area, and definitely some highly stylized floral pattern wallpaper—you're on your way.
- *Traditional:* Use classic pieces of quality English furniture, formal drapes, rich colors, and a cut-glass chandelier to accomplish this look.

▲ An elegant table in a room with a dramatic view may be all the decoration you need.

Formal Color

In the dining room, you can really experiment with your own tastes or get into a specific decorating style. The prominence of the dining room table and chairs allows you to use these pieces as the basis for the style you are looking to achieve. Unless you have something unusual like a red lacquered dining set (certainly possible for Asian décor), you won't be much limited in color choice.

If your plans for your dining room are very formal, you may want to look at bold floral wallpaper patterns, almost a must for the Victorian-style dining room. Or you can reserve the floral patterns for the draperies and instead paint the walls a warm, dark color. The formal dining room doesn't need a lot of ambient light unless you find the darker look more foreboding and depressing than romantic and elegant.

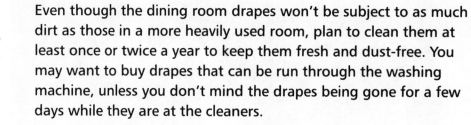

ALERT!

Even though the dining room drapes won't be subject to as much dirt as those in a more heavily used room, plan to clean them at least once or twice a year to keep them fresh and dust-free. You may want to buy drapes that can be run through the washing machine, unless you don't mind the drapes being gone for a few days while they are at the cleaners.

For a more modern look, a black-and-white dining room can be a lot of fun to put together. A black painted or metal table-and-chair against white walls contrast in a big way. Splashes of bold colors in the form of pottery, candlesticks, or even just the table settings or a large bouquet of bold flowers stands out against such a backdrop.

Windows and Lighting

Although windows are always nice, out of all the rooms in the house, windows are least important in the dining room. You can easily get away without windows in this room or with only small ones that don't open. This room has no upfront requirements, like the bathroom and kitchen do, for windows that provide ventilation. While you are dining, you are likely to use artificial light to create your own atmosphere anyway.

However, chances are your dining room does have some windows. So what do you do with them? Window treatments for the dining room can be lots of fun—flowing drapes and sheer liners can really add to the elegance of the room. Again, the dining room doesn't pose the design challenges of other rooms, where you have to worry about glare on a computer screen or a nice view while you are doing dishes, so go for whatever you like!

If your dining area is a nook off the open-concept dining room/ kitchen, café curtains may work well. Calico and gingham patterns are classic country style, but country doesn't have to be cute. More formal drapes can also be the backdrop for country furniture and accessories. Consider more rustic drapery hardware, such as wood or iron curtain rods with decorative finials, to help you create a comfortable country style.

Before you plan your décor, observe your dining room at all times of the day to get a sense of how the sun shines around the room. Place objects to take advantage of the sun, or not, depending on what you want to highlight. A highly ornate dining room can look lovely and soft in the sunlight.

Lighting in the dining room doesn't need to be fussy, but it is a serious consideration. A metal chandelier with bare candle-like bulbs is almost a prerequisite in the country dining room. Decide what effect you want lighting to have on the room. Is there a sitting area on one end or in one corner? This will need some task lighting for reading or ambient lighting for conversation.

◀ Nice chandeliers are popular for lighting a dining room.

Wonderful Walls

Unless your family is prone to food fights, you don't have to worry as much about washability and stain resistance when it comes to walls in the dining room as you do in the kitchen or bathroom, where grease splatters or mold and mildew accumulate.

Wallpapers in huge floral patterns are stunning for the dining room. They are also quite dramatic and prominent, so you'll want to enjoy their impact on a daily basis. Victorian décor would mix these patterns with floral elaborate draperies, but if you really want floral wallpaper to stand out, consider plain curtains in a complementary color.

Painted walls are also great in the dining room. If you have wainscoting on the lower part of the walls, paint that white and use the top portion of the walls to have fun. Or if you are really ambitious, sand the wainscoting down to bare wood. Finish the wood in stain or varnish and offset that with a warm palate-pleasing pastel. However, you'll want to keep in mind that if you have a wood dining table, it may be hard to match the wood wainscoting. Also, do a test patch behind a door or somewhere inconspicuous so you can see if the bare wood is nice enough to expose.

Dining Room Floors

Wood floors in the dining room are simply lovely. However, with the constant scraping of chairs as people sit at and get up from the table, you need to keep the floor protected.

A carpet under the table is one way—it is warm in winter and serves to protect the floor from the chair and table legs as well as shoe marks. However, it will need to be vacuumed often since food will surely be dropped with regularity onto the carpet.

Wood floors are great for decorating, as they offer a simple and natural backdrop to scatter rugs of any color and pattern you can find. Scatter rugs are also inexpensive and easy to change according to your whims.

If you'd like the look of wood but your family is tough on floors, you can get durability and looks from many of the simulated wood floorings on the market. The flooring industry has expanded its offerings tremendously, and there is a wide range of products on the market.

Linoleum isn't typically used in the dining room, but if your dining area is an alcove of the kitchen, this may be quite suitable. Ultimately, of course, you can do anything you want. So if you love linoleum, go for it!

FACT

Dimmer switches are perfect for the dining room. They allow you to light the room with plenty of versatility. You can go from a highly lit area for studying or doing close work at the table to a low-lit romantic table setting. It's not difficult to install a dimmer yourself, but you should be careful when replacing an existing light switch that also controls electrical outlets in the room. The dimmer knob must be on its highest setting to use anything other than lights at that outlet (vacuum cleaners or irons, for example). The dimmer should also be rated with enough power that it is able to safely handle all the wattage from those outlets combined with the lamp you want to dim. If the switch controls other outlets, it's probably best to get an electrician to install a separate switch for the dimmer.

Furniture as the Focal Point

Of course, the table is the premier piece of furniture in the dining room. If your dining room is strictly for dining, be very particular about the table. Find a table you want to live with for a long time.

You may already know if you want a round, square, or rectangular table. Round tables are nice in square spaces. Everyone dining faces each other, and there are no angles. At the same time, round tables tend to be used for more casual dining. If you do a lot of formal entertaining, therefore, you may want to opt for a rectangular table in the dining room and save the round table for the kitchen nook, eating porch, or deck.

If your budget allows, once you find a table you adore, buy other pieces to match it. Chairs are an obvious first. Choosing chairs can be complicated. The table may come with chairs, and by all means if you like them, you should match them up. But if there is something about the chairs that you don't particularly like, don't feel obligated to buy the set. Unless the table is of some unusual material, you will be able to find chairs that match even if you have to buy unfinished wood and match the stain of the table yourself.

Other furniture in the dining room may include side tables and buffets to hold extra food dishes, dessert, or perhaps a coffee urn. Depending on whether your dining room or kitchen has any built-in cabinets for good dishware, a hutch is always nice to show off special china that is reserved for special occasions or that is a family heirloom set.

If your dining area has a conversation nook, you will want to pick some comfortable chairs to furnish that. A nicely upholstered loveseat or a couple of wing chairs are perfect. Or, if the style of your dining room is heavily country or even Colonial, you might want a Windsor-style bench accompanied by a Windsor armchair for the conversation area. Make sure to have an end table nearby for a lamp and a place to set drinks or a plate of hors d'oeuvres.

Accessories

Setting the table is one of the most enjoyable decorating projects in the entire house. It takes little to create an elegant table setting.

Linens

If you don't have lots of sets of placemats, tablecloths, and matching napkins around, check the kitchen stores regularly for discounts on discontinued merchandise. Even if something is discounted because there is no longer a full set, a style of napkin and placement may sometimes come in varied colors. You can buy different colors and mix and match them.

Placemats are nice and, although somewhat informal, provide a nice way to show off a beautiful wood table and protect the wood at the same time. If you want to create a very formal dining table, choose a linen or damask tablecloth. All-white linen or damask is as elegant as any table gets. You can easily brighten up an all-white tablecloth with colorful dishware, candles, and flowers.

Lace doilies don't have to look old-fashioned. If they are antiques or your great grandmother's handiwork, you will want to leave them in their original state. But if they are bargains you picked up at a secondhand store, and they have no sentimental or antique value, get out some dye and try some wild colors to coordinate with the rest of your dining room décor. Purple or yellow lace will stand out nicely. Set vases and pitchers full of cut flowers on them, and let the touch of color peeking out around the edges pick up on a prominent color in the room.

Every three years or so, pull all of your dining room accessories out of the drawers and cupboards and assess your inventory. Toss things that are worn, and make note of what you want to replace. Take new color schemes into consideration and any new items you have added to your dining room décor.

Dishes

Glassware can make or break a table setting. Be sure glasses are spotlessly clean. You will want water glasses, wine glasses, and beer glasses on hand. They don't all have to be clear. A brightly colored water glass can add a nice flair to the table.

Candles

Candles finish off a dining room table setting in style. For formal elegant dining, choose tall smokeless, dripless tapers in classic colors like white, dark green, or red. For a more romantic and less formal look, scatter tea lights set in jelly jars or clear juice glasses—they are safe and the jars give off more light than the tea light actually provides on its own.

Don't use scented candles at the dining table. You don't want to overpower the scent of the food. Don't make your candles compete with your sumptuous-smelling meal.

FACT

For a basic table setting, set the napkin to the left of the plate with the salad fork and dinner fork on it. To the left of the napkin set the salad plate. The knife goes to the immediate right of the plate, and the spoon to the right of the knife. A glass for water, soda, or juice goes right above the knife and spoon. For more formal place settings, the rule is that the utensils are placed in the order they will be used, from the outside in. The fork for the first course would thus be on the farthest left. Utensils for the dessert course are placed horizontally above the plate (or they can be brought in with the dessert).

Flowers

A cut-flower arrangement is always a nice touch on the dining table. Keep a few different sizes of vases handy. A few bud vases with some wildflowers make a romantic table. Don't put an arrangement on the table that is so large your diners can't see each other. If you like a more dramatic vaseful of large, bold flowers, put that on a side table and let the wall color enhance the drama of the arrangement.

Mirrors

Mirrors are a natural candidate for dining room décor. As the feng shui information in the next section describes, they are particularly auspicious. For good décor, pick mirrors that reflect the style of your dining room. Don't use more than two mirrors total. Limit yourself to one significant mirror and one smaller one.

Feng Shui in the Dining Room

The dining room is an important place to take a look at energy flow and give a good feng shui assessment of this important room in the house.

Are you trying to lose weight? Good feng shui in the dining room leans toward avoiding the color black unless you are trying to shed a few pounds (although black is also considered very elegant).

If your dining room is close to the main door, concentrate on creating good feng shui with color and furnishings. This might include some feng shui fixes, such as mirrors and candles, so that dinner guests don't eat and run.

QUESTION?

What is a credenza?

Many furniture pieces have changed names over the years, and the credenza is a piece of dining room furniture that seems to have gone somewhat out of vogue. The credenza is used as a side table or buffet; one of its distinguishing features is that it has no legs but sits right on the floor. Typically a credenza has cabinet doors and perhaps a drawer for silver or napkin rings or other small dining table accessories.

Dining chairs should, of course, be comfortable. If you have a formal dining room and like to entertain, be sure to offer comfortable chairs that will encourage your dinner guests to relax and stay a while.

And lastly, mirrors in the dining room reflect or create the image of abundance, always good feng shui where food is concerned. (E)

Chapter 15
Living Rooms

The living room often serves very different purposes. Because we tend to do so many different things in this particular space, the living room is a well-used room in almost any home. For that reason, you'll want to keep it functional and enjoyable. There are many options for making this a room you'll love to live in!

Different Styles

Living rooms serve different purposes in different households. Some are focused around television viewing, while others are more formal and reserved mostly for company. Still other living rooms serve as quiet sitting areas reserved for reading, knitting, or listening to music.

It makes a lot of difference how you choose to decorate the room. Formal decorating is a lot of fun, but it can be frustrating to spend a great deal of time and money decorating a room that you rarely use.

Decorating for a more friendly, usable family room is still fun, but it requires a completely different approach. You will want to choose furnishings for comfort and durability first, style second.

The décor of the formal living room will probably be dictated by the decorating style you've chosen for the rest of the house. At the very least, a formal living room is used for company. This often means dinner guests, making it logical for the living room and dining room décor to be of the same (or in a similar) style. These rooms are most likely side by side in your home as well, so continuity in style is that much more important. Victorian, country, Arts & Crafts, traditional, modern—these styles and their offshoots (French country, cottage, and so on) are all common and wonderful styles to choose for decorating the living room.

FACT

If having furniture reupholstered is beyond your decorating budget, consider the next best thing: slipcovers. It may be difficult to find one for a unique piece that has an unusual shape, but you can also have them made at a cost that is still much less expensive than a full upholstering job. Slipcovers have the added advantage of being removable, so you can wash them.

In Living Color

Color schemes in the living room, whether formal or casual, should be relaxing. This is most likely a room where you will entertain guests, so you will want to carefully choose your main color and accent colors.

Colors should mesh from room to room. If you can see several rooms at once—for instance, dining room, foyer, and living room—you will want to keep in mind how the colors of these areas clash or go together. If each room is a different bright color, it will look like a rainbow running through your house. This can be cheerful, so go for it if it appeals to you! But it may also make the house seem rather busy.

Martha Stewart's line of paint, as well as others, offer great color chips that show color combinations in ranges. Some go from one color to a very different color. This kind of tool can be helpful in making decisions on color transitions that run from one room to the next. It can also be used to help with choices of more than just paint color. Use these chips to help you decide colors for accessories as well.

ESSENTIAL

> To start planning out your living room, grab a pencil and a piece of paper. Make a list of everything you already have that you want to include in the room. Note what color these things are. Decide what colors you want to enhance and what colors you wish would pretty much drop out of the picture. Then start to plan your full color scheme around the remaining pieces on your list.

Working with the Windows

Make your windows themselves beautiful to look at—whether the scene outside is beautiful or not—by using drapes of fabulous fabrics and patterns. Sheer liners add a simple touch of elegance to draperies. When privacy is an issue, such as with street-level windows, you can install roller blinds that can be rolled up out of the way during the times of day when privacy isn't a concern.

The curtains in your living room can be plain, or they can be elaborate enough to count almost as furnishings in their own right. Match them with floral fabric on throw pillows in the room or pick a simple, unpatterned fabric that picks up on a color in the floral upholstery of a chair and matching sofa.

Walls That Are Inviting

Are your living room walls broken up by lots of windows? Then you don't need to consider large expanses, which means you can choose almost anything to hang there. If wallpaper is your choice of wall decoration, however, keep in mind that lots of windows means a bit more complication when it comes to the wallpapering process.

The walls in the living room will probably be the backdrop for some paintings, pictures, or wall accessories. If you have pieces that you already know you want to hang in the living room, be sure to keep them in mind when you choose wall color. Black-and-white photos in simple black frames with white or off-white matting look good against almost any color wall. However, if you choose an abstract oil painting with a predominance of lime green and yellow to be the focal point of your living room, you may not want to paint the walls pink.

▲ In this living room, a brick fireplace is the focal point of the room.

If the walls are broken up with several windows, doorways, closet doors, a fireplace, gunstock corners, and other architectural details, don't feel like you have to hang something on every little piece of the wall. The details of the doorways and other features themselves already make the walls quite busy. Pick an interesting wall color, and let it show through in those small spaces.

On the other hand, if the walls aren't terrifically busy, sometimes a small painting, photo, or curio hung there can be fun. The key is not to overdo things so that in the midst of the crowd, nothing is noticeable anymore.

QUESTION?

Is there a classic traffic pattern for living rooms?
There is not as preset a traffic pattern for the living room as there is in the kitchen. However, since living rooms often accommodate the television, this focal point creates a need for specific traffic. First, consider distance. The television set should be several feet away from the seats intended for viewing, but not so far that the viewer feels like it's hard to concentrate. If a living room needs to do dual duty as a conversation area when you're entertaining guests, be sure to add a couple of seats that aren't necessarily facing the television.

Comfortable Floors

For a warm living room that you want to hang out in, carpeting is a must. Wall-to-wall is a typical way to go. Choose a simple color—tan or light green—that will match almost any décor. The expanse of a wall-to-wall carpet in a bright color is usually too much, although if you insist on it, the impact of the color can be lessened with large furnishings in more sedate colors or wood.

Arrange furniture so you can walk around it easily and not have to navigate through a maze to get to the easy chair. Carpets and runners provide good protection for much-traveled traffic patterns.

Lots of Lighting

For a living room that is used daily and for television viewing, you will want plenty of task lighting at the various sitting places in the room. Overall ambient lighting will probably interfere with the television screen, although it is always nice to have for cleaning any room.

Provide a table lamp for each side table, and a wall or floor lamp for every chair. Match all the lamps if your style is very formal. However, an eclectic grouping of lamps can be a lot of fun. The diversity can help add depth to a room through the different shapes and sizes of the bases and shades.

Recessed lighting in the living room can be great for ambient light. It can also serve the dual function of showcasing a fine piece of art, a porcelain collection, or even a beautiful built-in bookcase. Recessed lamps can fit any decorating style, but in a more modern décor, track lighting can serve the same purpose while adding to the contemporary feel of the room.

If your living room has a spectacular nighttime view from beautiful windows, allow for the lighting to be low so you can be sure to enjoy the view at night.

Of course, candles always create a lovely atmosphere. Candlesticks are perfect for a living room mantel. For a room without a fireplace, wall sconces can work just as well.

ALERT!

Although you don't want lighting to glare off the television screen, it is easier on your eyes if the television doesn't provide the only light in the room. Keep a floor lamp or table lamp in a good position to allow some light in the room. Be sure it is positioned so as not to reflect off the screen.

Furniture to Live In

If the living room in your home is the TV room, you will make some completely different choices when it comes to furnishings than you would if you used the room as a gathering place for guests.

If you have a rec room or family room, this is where the television really belongs. Décor is not enhanced by the blank television screen staring as you walk into the room. However, if it must go in the living room, there are several options for making it blend into the design scheme. Many pieces of furniture now exist to hide the television. For instance, you can buy an electronics cabinet in almost any furniture style. Even some of the finer woodworkers have recognized that homeowners who want handcrafted furniture have televisions and stereos that they would like to store in a fine piece of furniture that matches the rest of their furnishings. Country-style paneled cabinets abound in both the higher and lower end of electronics cabinets. However, more modern styles that consist mostly of glass and either wood or wood look-alikes are also easy to find. Taking a cue from hotels, you can find highboy mimics as well. In short, don't despair. If you want to hide the television, stereo, DVD player, all the requisite cable equipment, and their cords and wires, it can be done in almost any style you want.

▲ Large windows will make your living room feel more spacious.

Don't frustrate yourself with high-maintenance furniture in a room where the family kicks back with soda and chips to watch the ball game or your favorite sitcoms. Slipcover upholstered furniture, and pull the slipcovers off for regular cleanings. Buy chairs for comfort first, style second. Have enough seating for everyone in the family. Warm rugs and throw pillows also make casual relaxation areas, especially for kids.

If your living room is a formal room where you entertain guests, consider a conversation area as the central focus of the room. This may be organized around a sofa with matching chairs and/or loveseat. You can section off areas by simply arranging furniture at perpendicular angles instead of putting all your pieces against walls. If the room is small, however, don't frustrate people by making them try to walk around the furniture without tripping!

ESSENTIAL

Try using furniture in a different way. Just because a piece is intended for the dining room doesn't mean it wouldn't make a perfect addition to the living room. A side table that is supposed to be a buffet for beside the dining table might be just right behind the sofa if the sofa is used to section off an area of the living room.

Living rooms in England are called lounges. They are, by nature, rooms where people gather, whether it is just the family or a bunch of guests. While a decorating style of sparse furnishings and few accessories always looks neat and is easy to keep clean, if there is any room in your house that should be cozy and comfortable, this is the one—especially if you don't have the advantage of having a formal living room *and* a lounge/rec/family room.

Don't make this room so stiff and sparse that it simply isn't warm and inviting. Furnish it with good quality upholstered furniture flanked by places to set reading materials, a cup of tea, or a lamp. Scatter a couple of footrests, and hang some of your most enjoyable pieces of art.

If you have a favorite piece of upholstered furniture, perhaps one that holds some sentimental value, you can have it reupholstered to match the new décor or simply to freshen it up. However, upholstering can be expensive; sometimes even a small piece, like a loveseat, can require several yards of fabric. Before you spend the money on the upholstering, get a good assessment of the condition of the structure of the piece and be prepared for possible repairs and reinforcements that may be required.

Accessories

Coffee tables and end tables are a necessity in the living room. If you bought them with your sofa and matching chairs, you will have made it easy to match the side tables to the furniture. However, an eclectic approach is fine too.

Coffee tables can be a great place to have some fun using unusual things for a new purpose. Consider old trunks with flat, not rounded, tops. Or top an old wooden lobster trap from your vacation to New England with safety glass—you can decide whether a stuffed fuzzy lobster in the trap fits into your décor or not. Barrels, a thick piece of wood with the bark still on, or heck, even a couple of tires topped with glass can make a serviceable coffee table.

ALERT!

Candles in the living room make great atmosphere and are beautiful decorating accessories. However, unattended candles have also been responsible for many a house fire. Candles on the dining room table are usually the focus of the dinner table and all the diners. They aren't as easy to neglect as, say, a collection of candles on the coffee table in front of the sofa that keeps burning unattended when you get up, go to the kitchen for a beverage, and get distracted when the phone rings. If you have pets or children, candles on low surfaces are definitely unsafe. Also keep them away from drapes and plants. If you use candles frequently, consider keeping a miniature fire extinguisher tucked away in the closet or behind the door.

As mentioned earlier, in the casual living room, big pillows for lounging on warm rugs are a must. Throw pillows can offset color schemes. If you have fine furniture and want to keep the surfaces free of rings from wet drink glasses, make sure there are always plenty of coasters in prominent places to remind guests and family to use them.

For a living room that sees a lot of lounging, lap blankets are useful. If you'd rather they not end up in a heap at the end of the sofa or draped over chairs, place a trunk in the room that's especially meant to hold blankets and pillows when the room is tidied up. The trunk can serve dual purpose as an end table, but don't place anything "permanent" on it, like a lamp or piece of decorative pottery. You don't want to discourage tidying up by making the trunk difficult to open because the top has to be cleared first.

A globe or map is a nice accessory, especially for a room focused on television viewing. Many globe companies even offer regular replacements as the countries of the world change.

Books are great accessories in any room; in the living room, you can plan to store your oversized art, garden, architecture, and other books that are decorating pieces in and of themselves. Make sure there is a nice chair nearby to relax into with one of these oversized books. You might also consider a dictionary stand. This is not only a wonderful decorative item but a practical place to keep that huge dictionary that you would refer to more often, if only it were accessible.

FACT

In mid-nineteenth-century New England, artists traveled the countryside, making a living painting murals on the walls of homes and public buildings as they went. The artwork of these itinerant muralists still graces many walls to this day. Perhaps your living room has a wall that would be perfect for a great mural. If you are artistic, you might try painting it yourself! If not, there are artists around today who specialize in painting murals on walls. Check with your local art association and ask if they can recommend any artists who paint wall murals.

Feng Shui in the Living Room

How does your living room's energy shape up? Here are some things to consider to help with the feng shui balance in this social room.

Round shapes help good chi circulate through the house, and the living room is a great place to include things of this shape. Try a round rug, ottoman, coffee table, or even a rounded overstuffed chair.

A room that is used mainly for guests should offer ready access to the house and so should be near the front door of the house. Additionally, south is the best direction for the living room to face, although there are no dire consequences from a living room that faces any other direction.

Fireplaces are great, but in feng shui practice, you always want to be concerned about places where chi can flow out of the room too easily. As with all energy flow, this energy depletion can be fixed by rechanneling energy using mirrors, wind chimes, crystals, flutes, and other feng shui fixes. Ⓔ

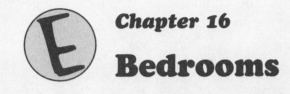

Chapter 16

Bedrooms

Bedrooms are the perfect place to stretch your decorating creativity to its limits. These rooms are where you want to be at your most relaxed and comfortable. Guests won't typically see this room, so you don't need to feel forced into matching the décor in the rest of the house. However, whatever you do choose, you'll want to be sure that the general approach is in keeping with the intent of the room—relaxation and romance.

Stylish Bedrooms

Almost any style goes in the bedroom, but a cozy nest in the Victorian style can make this private room quite romantic. However, if the clutter of this style doesn't work for you, a minimalist modern or Shaker-style bedroom décor can also be very relaxing. Country style and cottage style offer great possibilities for the bedroom as well, with great bed designs and linens available to set the stage.

Soothing Colors

Grays and greens are peaceful, restful colors suitable for the room you sleep in. Wild patterns and crazy wallpaper are fine. But with those surrounding you, don't be surprised if you don't feel like letting out that big relaxing sigh when you finally hit your bedroom at the end of a long day!

If you do want that kind of decorating in your bedroom, consider papering just one wall and painting the rest. Or use touches of bold fabrics in a throw pillow or decorative edges on plain curtains. This can bring some fun and distinction to a bedroom without overwhelming it.

Windows and Lighting

Heavy drapes in the bedroom can not only create a romantic and cozy décor but can also can help block out street noise if your bedroom windows face out onto a busy street. Drapes can also easily accommodate undertreatments of sheer curtains or blinds that allow for some privacy, even when the drapes are open.

Bedsheets make dreamy and appropriate drapes or curtains in the bedroom. They give you the added advantage of being able to match your curtains and bed linens perfectly, no matter how unusual the pattern.

You probably always want to have the option of opening the drapes and the windows in the bedroom. Even if all you want is just to air the room and to leave the windows closed while you are sleeping, fresh air is still vital.

Although every room should have a ceiling light or some other way to light up the whole room for cleaning and perhaps for the rare occasions that you move things around, most bedroom lighting can focus on task lighting.

First and foremost, be sure there are reading lamps on each side of the bed. Even those people who wouldn't describe themselves as "readers" most likely often relax with a magazine or newspaper before falling asleep. Also, the reading lamps should be easily reached from the bed. No one likes to have to get out of bed to shut the light off. Reading lamps do not need to be too faithful to any particular decorating style. They usually can be found in quite simple styles to fit with almost any look you've chosen.

If you want or need—because of space concerns—to have a work space in the bedroom, consider disguising it by partitioning off the work area behind a dressing screen or curtains.

Other task lights include dressing areas and around bureaus and dressers. Lights around the dresser can help you avoid having to put clean clothes away in the dark or having to walk across the room to decide if a pair of socks is blue or black.

You may also have a reading chair in the bedroom, and if so, a light will certainly be needed there. Also consider some ambient lighting to create a soft, moody atmosphere.

Wall Coverings

Except for kids' rooms that are also used for play, bedrooms have the luxury of few requirements for wear and tear—they don't have to withstand heavy soiling such as grease in the kitchen or dirty hands in the bathroom. You can more easily get away with at least a satin finish paint. Even flat paint would be fine. In a relaxing room like a bedroom, avoiding the high shine of semigloss paint is desirable.

The same goes for wallpaper. Where kitchens and bathrooms (especially) and other rooms in the house need to hold up to lots of potential dirt and grime, bedrooms aren't as susceptible. Therefore, you can use almost any type of wallpaper and not be limited to patterns that come in practical, washable vinyl. Brocade-type wallpaper and relief patterns are a go in the bedroom!

Floors That Relax

Carpeting is the most common bedroom floor covering, perhaps because we associate the sleeping area with soft and quiet things. In cottage or seaside styles, it is not unusual for the bedrooms to have painted floors. A painted floor can signal cool and airy, like the natural environment of a seaside setting. Don't overlook the idea of making painted floors unique—faux patterns are very suitable for floors and can be so complex as to resemble linoleum.

Bedroom Furniture

On first consideration, people think mainly of the bed when they think of bedroom furniture. However, the bedroom can be host to many possible furnishings. Let's start with the first bed and then move on to other, more minor but still common, bedroom furniture.

◀ A valence over the bed is an unusual and dramatic variation on a headboard.

The Bed

It's fairly evident that the bed is typically the focal point in any bedroom. While many of us started our adult lives with the mattress-on-the-floor routine, graduating first to a mattress on a box spring on the floor and then to the addition of a simple metal bed frame, at some point almost all of us choose to have a complete bed frame.

You will focus on the headboard when making your selection for a full bed frame. You'll need to consider size and style when looking at headboards.

As with any furniture purchase, have some measurements with you when you head out to pick your bedframe. The actual room dimensions will matter only in choosing whether you get a king, queen, or full-size mattress. But no matter what the bed's "footprint," from a decorating standpoint, the headboard can either overwhelm, enhance, or blend with the room's overall décor. You won't want to choose a headboard that is huge and heavy looking if the rest of the room is decorated delicately.

FACT

Dormers are little cutouts in the roof line on the second floor that create a bit more space and a lot more light in a house with a large expanse of roof. Dormers create great little nooks in bedrooms and can be lots of fun to decorate. Of course, installing one is a remodeling project, not a decorating project, but you might already have a dormer window or be having one or two built. If so, shop the secondhand stores for just the right piece of furniture. You might also have a window seat built right in. In either case, create cushions with fabric to match the rest of the room, hang a plant or a little set of paintings on one side, and you will have a cozy little space that can make an otherwise plain bedroom quite unique!

Headboards will come in three basic materials: wood, metal, or upholstery. All three can offer very different styles. Wood headboards can be heavy looking in dark grain or stain, carved, or otherwise ornately put together. Depending on the ornamentation, this would be a good choice for a Far Eastern or Victorian décor. Wood offers the widest range of choice. You can select from pencil post beds, Shaker style, or Mission style, for instance. Some combinations of materials also work well—wood frames with rattan weave, or wood and upholstery.

If you are going for a contemporary or sparse look, a metal frame will do the trick nicely. Metal frames can also be more ornate, but the look can still be contemporary against a boldly painted wall. Brass beds are very Victorian and can be rather simple or rather flamboyant.

ALERT!

Canopies aren't for everyone, but they do create a magical atmosphere in the bedroom. If you don't have or aren't inclined to get a classic canopy bedframe, you can create your own. Attach rings or other holders to the ceiling at the four corners of the bed and hang fabric from each; drape fabric in between the hooks at the ceiling and voilà! You have a quick and inexpensive canopy. It is also quickly dismantled, although you may have to patch the ceiling if you choose to take down the rings. (For safety reasons, this is not an appropriate decorating idea for a child's room!)

Creating the Headboard Look

If you have a mattress and box spring on a simple metal frame and aren't interested in a full-fledged bed frame, you can create the look of a headboard in many ways. This will give the bed area a more "finished" feel. The simplest way of all would be an elaborate use of pillows—large comfortable pillows or oversized bolsters can be the backdrop with smaller sleeping pillows layered in front. Keep a trunk at the end of the bed, and at night, slip the decorative pillows into the trunk.

A more prominent handcrafted headboard is to hang a curtain rod up on the wall behind the head of the bed and create a headboard effect out of layered draperies. Cap the drapes with a valence to pull the effect together. This can be very dreamy, with layers of ornate fabrics, for a more Victorian décor, but it can also fit into a more modern décor with the right fabric and less layering.

If the curtains extend to the bedframe, be sure that when a person leans back against them, they won't be likely to pull the whole thing down on their head. The curtain rod needs to be tightly secured and the drapes not easily ripped from the rod.

Platform Beds

Platform beds are bed frames that create a solid platform for a mattress to set on. The useful characteristic of a platform bed is that under the platform, around the perimeter of the bed, there are usually several built-in drawers for convenient storage for linens, blankets, or seasonal clothing.

Bunk Beds

Bunk beds in kids rooms are always a fun element. Just be sure they actually will fit before you buy! Look for ones with all the modern safety features with easy-to-climb ladders and railings around the top bunk. And teach kids how to use them safely.

Tables

The most important table to consider in the bedroom is the bedside table. If the bedroom is used by a couple, there should definitely be a side table on each side of the bed, or magazines, newspapers, and books will stack up on the floor. Lounging with the Sunday newspaper and coffee is a whole lot easier with a side table to put your coffee on, and the table also serves to lessen the chance of a cup tipping over and staining the bed linens.

Bedside tables can be equipped with a drawer to hold small items like a pair of reading glasses, hand cream, or jewelry, and a shelf below the drawer is convenient for storing books and magazines that you dip into occasionally before bed. If the table is big enough, then tabletop bedside lamps will work. If the tabletop is small, keep that space clear for other things and hang wall reading lamps on each side of the bed.

If your bedroom is big enough, consider a small sitting table as part of the décor. Tables layered in heavy, long fabric topped with a lacy tablecloth can add to a romantic Victorian look. If the table is a lovely wood, let the wood shine through and use coasters and doilies. Equip the table with a couple of cozy chairs, and you've got a romantic, quiet reading or writing nook.

FACT

Rope beds were the norm in colonial times. These beds typically were made with fairly large timbers for frames, sometimes with headboards and foot boards, sometimes with just the four corner posts. The trick of the rope bed was that the mattress—probably a thin ticking stuffed with straw or feathers—was supported by a lacing of manila rope. The rope was strung through holes in the bedframe. It was carefully twisted and tightened in order to comfortably suspend the mattress and the weight of the person sleeping on it.

Dressers

Dressers are a key furniture item in the bedroom. An essential part of successful home decorating is keeping clutter at bay, and the best way to do that is to have a place for everything. Dressers help with the task of keeping your clothes clean, folded, and out of the way.

Vanity

Vanities are traditionally a woman's furniture item that recall an age of more elaborate lifestyles. In this age of casual dress and fast paces, they aren't as common as they once were. A full vanity with a large mirror, middle drawer, and perhaps a couple of raised shelves on either side of a built-in drawer is a great piece to add to a Victorian-style bedroom. The right vanity can also help relieve the bathroom of some clutter and house your makeup, hairbrushes, and other grooming supplies.

Some contemporary bedroom suites come with a matching vanity, so don't despair. If this is a piece of bedroom furniture that you can't live without, you can get it to match. You will need a relatively large bedroom to comfortably accommodate a vanity.

Chairs

Again, depending on the size of your bedrooms, chairs are nice items of furniture to have there. If this is where your clothes are and therefore where you change, it is convenient to be able to sit in a chair to take off or put on shoes and socks. A cozy upholstered chair is a welcome spot in a room as private as the bedroom—perhaps if you can retreat to the bedroom to just sit and collect your thoughts, you can get a little undisturbed time of peace and quiet!

◄ Create a sitting area in a bedroom with a couple of comfortable chairs and a table with a reading lamp.

One common laundry problem is what to do with the item that has been worn but isn't really dirty and could be worn again before washing. Designate a chair to accommodate these clothes. Fold jeans and put in the seat, drape shirts over the back. If you make it officially your "in-between laundry chair," you will have a place to put these clothes. You also won't be frustrated that the chair can't be used for sitting because you never intended it for that use anyway.

Sometimes chairs in the bedroom can simply be decorative. Maybe the fabric is lovely, the chair is an antique, the wood deep and rich, or the woodworking just something you enjoy admiring.

ALERT!

Keep your bedroom as simple as possible. Nothing should discourage you from keeping this room extra clean. Clean, dust-free air is best for the place you sleep. Many people like to sleep with their pets, but pets in the bedroom, or even worse on the bed itself, are a quick way to make a bedroom difficult to keep clean.

Armoires

Another item that needs space but that can help tremendously in the case of houses that don't have lots of closet space—especially older houses—is the armoire. Armoires often are just empty cabinets that you use to hang clothes. Some armoires come with a vertical column of drawers for lingerie, sweaters, and other small items, with just half the armoire suitable for hanging items. They may even include a large drawer or two across the bottom.

Armoires can be heavy pieces of furniture with large expanses of surface. Decoratively carved armoires can be real signature pieces when incorporated in a Far East decorating style. Even cottages can accommodate an armoire, especially if they are decorated in light colors such as white or light blue. On a painted armoire, you may want to break up the surface with some stenciling or decorative painting techniques.

Consider your room carefully before choosing an armoire. If you have no closet space, it may be a decision of practicality. If you are simply charmed by armoires, be cautious of whether the size of your room can really accommodate it. An armoire can be either a significant decorative enhancement or a white elephant.

Accessories

Accessories are where decorating can get its most creative and where you can really express your personal style. After the overall style, accessories make your look. This goes beyond the difference between baskets and gingham for a traditional country look or brightly glazed pottery and geometric patterns for a modern look. Accessories handcrafted by you or crafted by a master artisan also adds to the style.

If you are handy with a sewing machine, glue gun, and other craft-related tools, you can have loads of fun making projects from patterns and kits or designing accessories of your own.

Think about making your bedroom décor easily changeable with the changing of seasons. Changing furniture slipcovers, throw rugs, curtains, and bed linens can easily transform a bedroom from summer light to winter warm.

Mirrors

Don't forget mirrors when it comes to accessories. Rooms can be transformed by mirrors, and mirrors are a natural for the bedroom. They don't have to be in traditional frames—think outside the box. Consider old window frames, discarded large wood dies from an industrial plant, or elaborate frames that formerly held paintings or photos.

If your bedroom is also where you dress, you will of course want a full-length mirror available here. It can be a simply framed mirror that you attach to the back of the bedroom door. More charming, if you have the space, is the self-standing mirror that has a frame and a stand of some kind. These can be perfect in a Victorian setting, but they are also now made in a variety of styles to fit any décor. You just need the floor space—you don't want to put your full-length mirror in a spot where it is constantly covered up.

Vanity mirrors usually come attached to the dresser part of the vanity. If you buy a mirrored vanity, you can be sure that the mirror and the dresser match. However, if your bedroom is more of a mishmash of styles, you can create your own vanity out of a low table or a writing desk and attach a mirror to the wall above the table. Paint them the same color and you'll find that the two pieces are almost indistinguishable from a single piece!

If you go the two-piece route, use the mirror to add to the atmosphere by placing it low enough to the table to reflect lovely perfume bottles, a colored vase that you keep filled with fresh flowers, and other items that look beautiful once and even better twice when reflected back from the mirror!

Bed Linens

Linens, like the bed itself, are one of the most prominent decorating presences in a bedroom. Buy the best linens you can afford. Cheap sheets are hard to keep in place on the bed because the elastics of the fitted sheet quickly lose their elasticity. Inexpensive linens also make for a less all-around polished look to the bedroom.

Be sure to pick a fabric that you will be comfortable to sleep in. Just because silk sheets look elegant doesn't mean you will like sleeping on them! Flannel sheets have come a long way in the past twenty years, and you can now buy great flannel sheet designs if you like the warm feel during the winter months.

If you've graduated to the "real bed" phase of your home decorating life, consider a bed ruffle. A ruffle can finish off a luxurious bedroom look and has the practical advantage of reducing the dust that makes it under the bed, as well as hiding anything stored under there.

Besides your sleeping pillows, some big pillow shams can also polish off the look, but don't bother with them if you have no place to put them at night and always have them tossed on the floor.

Once you've gone to all the trouble of creating a lovely bed in a lovely bedroom, be sure to make your bed every day and enjoy your fabulous linens!

Pillows

Throw pillows are a great accessory for any room where you do some relaxing. Pillow covers can be easily changed to match the other fabrics in the room or offset the wall color. They are easy to make, and if you put a zipper in them they are just as easily washed.

If you really want to jazz up the pillows and the space, add a little lace to the edge or appliqués on the front. Pillows are such a manageable size that pillow covers come together fast. You can use great fabric since you don't need a lot, so feel free to get creative!

QUESTION?

What is a trundle bed?
Trundle beds roll out from underneath a main bed. They are often used by children. Before central heating, beds often were put in the living room to be near the warmth of the main hearth or for their use as dual-purpose furniture—sleeping at night, lounging in the day or evening—so a trundle bed allowed for the space to be cleared for daytime activities.

Artwork

A painting as a focal piece in the bedroom is a great way to offset the prominence of the bed. Pick something you really enjoy looking at and will be comforting and soothing before you turn off the light.

If your bedroom has a large wall, use it to hang a large painting. Frames can be found in every size and shape imaginable, so you can select something that will match or offset the rest of the bedroom easily. Consider also hanging a group of photos or other artwork if you don't have a piece large enough to hang alone on a large expanse of wall. Framing art in matching or similar frames will give the pieces a cohesive look that will make a great focal point.

Trunks

Trunks from the old days of ship travel are quite good finds and easy to restore and use as furniture items. A trunk can do dual service as a storage place for off-season linens or clothing and a small tea table in a bedroom.

Be careful of the inside, though. Air them out thoroughly or buy a new chest or trunk that has cedar or some natural moth- and must-controlling quality.

Quilts

Quilts are a natural for a bedroom, but they don't have to be used just on the bed! Quilts make great wall hangings or even table linens. If you use antique quilts, be careful to put them where sunlight can't hit them. In fact, any fabric is adversely affected by the sun, so place them according to how important it is to you that they last a long time. Don't give up the family heirloom to the sun.

Feng Shui in the Bedroom

Before you get started decorating your bedroom and after you think you are finished, give the room a little feng shui review:

- Are mirrors placed to prevent surprises and to help chi flow smoothly around the room?
- Is your bed placed diagonally opposite of the entrance, that is, out of alignment with the door so it does not obstruct the energy path and so that you are not in a position of easy access to heaven?
- If the head of your bed has to be below a window, do you have something between the bed and the window—a shelf, a chair—that can slow down the chi so that it doesn't just go through your body and right out the window?
- If your bedroom is not in the southwest corner of the house—the compass direction that controls partnerships—have you enhanced that area of the room with good energy directors like crystals or a bamboo flute?
- Is your bedroom painted in colors conducive to sleeping and rest and void of clutter as well as the electromagnetic fields of electronics like televisions and computers?

Good feng shui and a fun décor can make your bedroom your favorite room in the house! Ⓔ

Chapter 17

Kids' Rooms

The rooms for the children in your home do not have to be a challenge. Instead, they can be the most fun rooms to decorate of all! Needs and likes vary drastically among different age groups, of course. This chapter will help you focus on what to consider and what options you have when decorating rooms for the kids in your life.

Preparing for Baby

Preparing the nursery is a time-honored ritual, and the decorative items available for this room are as varied as your imagination. The crib and changing area will, out of sheer practicality, be the focus of attention of the infant's room. You need to make the room both efficient and practical. For the first year or so you don't even have to be concerned with what the child thinks of the room, except for providing great visual stimulation in the form of mobiles, novelty lamps, and other fun things for baby to look at from the crib. But be sure to make the room comfortable and enjoyable for you and the baby's other adult caretakers since for that first eighteen months, the room is really yours.

Since the adult user of an infant's room will probably either be soothing the baby to sleep or changing a diaper, there are really just a couple of basic needs for this room.

- Paint the walls in a soft, relaxing color. If you are going to sit and rock a baby to sleep, you will want to be able to relax and pass that along to the child.
- Make room for a comfortable chair—you will probably be spending quite a bit of time in it.
- Don't jam the room full of stuff. Keep the diaper-changing area clear of clutter so you can always get to it and not trip over things with a baby in your arms.
- Have the crib in a space where there are no dangers nearby like electrical outlets, tables with lamps on them, or near a window blind with a pull cord.

Use moveable and transformable things like colorful plastic crates and knockdown furniture to decorate kids' rooms. These elements can be easily moved around or moved out as your child gets older.

From there, you can decorate to your tastes. The array of fabrics with fun designs is endless, and it's great fun to shop for material to make lightweight, simple curtains for an infant's room. Tie them back with old-fashioned diaper pins or bendable rattles. Edge them with pompom trim. The name of the game is fun!

The Toddler and the Preschooler

Kids who are on the move create a whole new set of challenges and opportunities for decorating (not to mention the challenges of decorating the rest of the house). First, the room will now need to accommodate a bigger bed. Perhaps this can easily be done by moving the crib out. Or it may require moving or removing other furniture in the room.

If you got into the pale pink or baby blue color scheme for the infant, now is the time to ditch those. This does not mean that pink and blue can't show up somewhere. But at this age, a child's mind is expanding rapidly. You need to pick stimulating colors that will tone down for sleeping when the room is lit only with a nightlight.

If your child is lucky enough to have his or her own bathroom, be sure it follows all safety standards. Encourage the child to keep the bathroom clean and tidy to help avoid falls and other accidents.

One mother of three toddlers was pretty clear that at that age, "storage, storage, storage" is the key. The big question is whether your child's room serves as the main play area. If so, toy storage is a big consideration. If not, the playroom probably has plenty of storage, although kids will always want some toys in their room. Just be sure there are places to put them. You want to prevent your child from tripping over them on late-night visits to the bathroom, and you also want the room obstacle-free when you tiptoe in to check on them.

Storage Ideas

Things to use for storage are limited only by your imagination. However, do not use items that kids can lock themselves into or otherwise get trapped in.

Toy Chest

Toy chests have always been favorites, and most grown-up kids have fond memories of their toy chests. You don't need to be a woodworker to create a personalized toy chest. Check out any unfinished furniture outlet, and you will surely find a couple of styles to choose from. Paint them to match the room, stencil them with farm animals or zoo animals, or decoupage clippings from magazines of your kids' favorite things—like tractors, trains, horses, or fire trucks. Stencil your child's name on the chest, and no matter how fancy or how simple the construction, it will be a treasure for life.

Plastic Containers

A couple of the major plastic manufacturers have designed dozens of lidded storage containers. Containers range in size, from small containers suitable for holding crayons, to bigger containers capable of holding an expansive Lego collection. These usually have handles, making them transportable, so after the living room floor has been used as the play area for the afternoon, small toys can go back in their plastic storage bins and be easily toted back to the child's room.

They even make plastic storage bins that roll, usually designed as a stack of multiple bins of varying sizes on casters. You can place these containers side by side until the child gets older and then these can be stacked one on top of another. Get clear ones so you can see what is in them.

Another perennial favorite in the plastic department are square or rectangular crates. Again, these are sized small so they hold just enough that they can still be toted around. They are also stackable.

The Preteen Room

Now you are getting into serious decorating business. If you really enjoy decorating, you will be able to have a blast with the preteen room. Kids at this age have distinguishing tastes and have typically developed hobbies around which you can create a decorating scheme.

Wall Décor

Let the preteen child pick the color scheme for his or her room. If you are worried that the choice won't suit you, go to the paint store and gather chips in the colors of their liking. Pick two or three possibilities that you could live with and give the child that choice. This is a great way to start kids thinking about style and learning about decorating.

▲ Make use of fun wallpaper borders to spruce up the décor in kids' rooms.

Although wallpaper is great in kids' rooms and there is an endless selection of fun designs, wallpaper is not as easy to install as paint is to put on. It therefore doesn't afford as much do-it-together decorating opportunity as paint does. If you decide on paper, consider doing the woodwork together first, and then take over the actual wallpapering, finding ways for your preteen to help.

Furniture

If the preteen's bed itself isn't ornate, you can dress it up a lot with bed linens and bedspreads and pillow shams. Again, the choices are endless. Chances are good that you can find something that is in keeping with the room's color scheme or the child's hobby or sport of choice.

Space will probably need to be carved out in the room for doing homework and studying, especially for the older preteen. Computers are pretty much now standard equipment in a room for kids of this age (unless you prefer to keep the computing to a more open place where you can at least partially monitor what they are doing online). A desk is standard, but that piece of furniture for a kid this age doesn't have to be oh-so-serious.

This is probably a little early for serious stereo equipment; a typical boombox or portable CD player will have no problem fitting in some-where. However, CD storage might be something to think about. CD towers and other types of shelving have become quite stylish.

Bookshelves will be a necessity in the preteen room. Kids may still enjoy a peek once in a while at their all-time favorite picture books. Books for schoolwork and chapter books for reading should also be assigned some designated space to keep them neat.

A night table with a reading lamp and maybe a drawer for a diary is always appreciated next to the bed.

Unfinished furniture pieces are a great choice for kids' rooms. They can easily be painted in bright colors and are inexpensive enough that you won't mind if they get covered with stickers or written on with markers. When the kids outgrow them, you can easily paint over them and use them elsewhere or sell them in a yard sale.

Guests

Is your preteen prone to hosting sleepovers and slumber parties? Is her or his room set up for this kind of additional occupancy? Kids don't mind sleeping on the floor in sleeping bags, but if the room doesn't have a lot of floor space left over after accommodating furnishings, you need to be able to easily move some furniture out of the way. Cots and air mattresses are also great temporary sleeping spaces, and they can be easily stored away after the slumber party is over.

Decorating for Two in a Room

If kids in your home share a room, you will want to decorate for privacy. Here are some ideas:

- Take some tips from college dorm rooms. Use space-efficient furniture and create two distinct areas that are mirror images of each other, including bed, desk, bulletin board, and shelving for whatever the child likes to collect—whether that's dolls, cars, games, or art supplies.
- Create temporary privacy using dressing screens, or turn bookcases back to back to create partial walls.
- Use lighting imaginatively to create two separate areas of the room.
- If the kids have different tastes when it comes to color, give them some color combinations that complement each other, then let them each paint their respective areas of the room in the colors they prefer. If that's too much for you to deal with, let one child pick the main color and the other pick the color of the trim and soft furnishings, like curtains, rugs, and bedspreads.

The preteen bedroom doesn't have to be just plain painted walls and a few stuffed animals. Consider making the room look like a big aquarium (but no sharks!). If your preteen is horse crazy but you have no plans to get a real one, you can create a room that is a pretend stable. Try creating a scene from your child's favorite picture book. Or simply stencil fun quotes on brightly painted walls—kids need all the inspiration they can get!

The preteen's tastes will change rapidly anyway, so whichever of these ideas you choose, you can be sure it won't be around for a long, long time—maybe for just long enough that you both tire of it.

Safety Concerns

The child's room should be a safe place for a kid to sleep and play. You can work on childproofing the room yourself, or you can hire a childproofing expert as a consultant. The expert will go through your entire home and point out everything you need to do to make your home safe for children. Many of these consultants charge a nominal fee and make their money selling the products that they recommend to help you make your home safe.

Another possibility is the franchise company Safety Matters (check out their Web site at *www.safetymatters.com* or call 1-800-9SAFE06). Although a lot of the information on the company Web site is about babies, it is worth a visit for parents of older children, too. You'll find a "walk thru tips" section that walks through a typical home and points out over a dozen areas to check out for safety issues. And you can order products from the site, including safe-baby gates and outlet plates with built-in safety plug covers. (The kind you pop in, although difficult for children to remove, pose a choking hazard if a persistent child did manage to remove one.)

Bunk Beds

Kids love bunk beds, and in a room that is shared by two kids, bunk beds can be almost a necessity. However, they pose some real safety concerns. Keep all assembly instructions and use everything provided for their assembly. Install the guardrail for the top bunk, and securely attach the ladder. The safety regulations that the manufacturers are required to follow are only as good as your adherence to them.

The manufacturer tries to ensure that the person on the bottom bunk can sit up without hitting her or his head on the top bunk. You need to make sure that the bunk beds are set up in a room with a ceiling high enough for the kid in the top bunk to sit up safely, too.

Tips to Avoiding Accidents

Do not have locks that work from the inside of the room in kids' rooms or closets. Install double locks if you really want locks on these doors, so that you can unlock the door from either side in case a child locks herself in her room or a bathroom.

Keep electrical outlets covered, either using the small plastic covers that you can pick up in a hardware store or the larger baby stores, or by completely replacing the wall plate with a special safety plate that covers the plugs when they are not in use.

Don't use high bureaus in kids' rooms unless you secure them to the wall. Kids can't reach the top drawers. At the toddler and preschool age, they are by nature becoming a little more independent. They could be seriously injured if a dresser tipped over on top of them as they attempted to get to the top drawer. Keep tipping dangers in mind for other independent storage furniture as well, in the child's room or elsewhere in the house.

ESSENTIAL

Does good feng shui matter when it comes to children? You bet! The colors of education and knowledge are black, blue, and green. Use these colors to enhance your child's studying and homework. Keep in mind all the things about a bedroom that can enhance the flow of chi—no poison arrows (that is, sharp furniture edges) aimed at the bed, and the bed placed off to the side so that it is not in line with the doorway and windows, allowing chi to flow easily in and out of the room.

Toxic and nontoxic materials are a concern to consider throughout your home, but if you have children around, you must be especially careful in their rooms. Avoid wall-to-wall carpeting with glues that create noxious outgassing. Use materials that don't require special toxic cleaners to maintain them. Railings are a classic place where kids' heads or limbs get stuck. Have a safety expert help you decide the appropriate kind of railings to use if your home has an open stairwell.

No matter what you are buying, if it is going to end up in a child's room, read the manufacturers' labels carefully. Manufacturers are under strict federal guidelines to warn consumers about potential child safety issues with their products. Check *Consumer Reports* or the U.S. Consumer Products Safety Commission (*www.cpsc.gov*) often to see what products have been recalled for safety issues.

Other areas around the home to specifically consider when thinking about safety are kitchens, bathrooms, and pools. Think about things like pet doors and holiday decorations—are they safe for the kids?

The Teenager's Room

Here is the place to give up. Teens want colors you never imagined would be painted on a wall, and they want space for stereo equipment. And a cordless phone. The rest is mostly excess!

This is, of course, a grand stereotype, and many teens love to decorate their rooms. So let them! It is a great learning tool for when, in the not-too-distant future, they will be decorating dorm rooms, apartments, and then their own houses. Why not start letting them learn about good decorating now? Just remember that doesn't mean forcing your decorating style on them. Your job is to guide them toward good choices that they won't regret later.

FACT

A bulletin board is always a great addition to a kid's room. Hang the largest board the room can accommodate—it offers an automatic decorating space that the kids can change as often as they like. A bulletin board also can serve as a perfect catch-all for those items that have nowhere else to go, like a bird's feather or a trinket from a birthday party.

Encourage them to use fabrics and throw pillows and other easily changed things so they can redecorate often and inexpensively. They probably also need some good lessons in decorating in a way that can be easily cleaned around.

Teens, of course, need some studying space. Even if they painted the walls black, be sure there is good lighting around a desk area. Again, bookcases are a must, even if they are temporary types like plastic crates (maybe salvaged from the old days when they stored toys in them as toddlers—that plastic doesn't just go away).

Chapter 18
Other Rooms

Extra rooms in your home don't have to be an afterthought. They can, however, be great places to collect pieces that don't quite fit anywhere else in the house. Many homes have space for a home office and a guest room, and some even offer their occupants the luxury of having a private library, a separate laundry room, or even a year-round conservatory or sunroom. The key consideration when decorating these rooms is functionality.

The Occasional Office

The intensity with which you tackle a home office is directly proportional to the amount of time it is used. A home office that is used every day for the at-home worker will have significantly more complex decorating requirements than the home office that is for Saturday morning bill paying, once-a-month budget review, and a few hours a week of Internet surfing.

Most likely the occasional office is the place where the household bills are stored and paid. The key piece of décor will be a desk of some kind. The size of your space will dictate this to some degree—if your home office is no more than a nook at the end of the hall off the kitchen, buy a desk to fit. If you can't get a desk that will fit in the size of the space, make one out of a couple of file cabinets on either side and a piece of wood to rest on top. Make sure the wood is smooth, like a luan door or high-grade plywood, with the edge you will be sitting against finished smooth. You might even cover this edge with molding to keep it from hooking your sweater or scratching your arms.

You don't need to leave the makeshift desktop as is. You can paint it, cover it with fabric, add a large writing pad, and you will have an attractive work surface. Much of the rest of it will be covered with pen holders and other office supplies, as well as your computer.

ESSENTIAL

Decorating with office-related things is fun. Artwork from computer parts, for example, is right at home in this setting. Pick fun pieces that are functional—a clock face set in a polished beach stone, a favorite piece of Fiestaware for a pen holder, or a calendar showcasing pictures of your favorite antique boats.

Another convenient item is a bill organizer. The way you are most comfortable organizing your bills will determine the type of organizer that will suit your needs. If your desktop is big enough to fit it, you can buy attractive organizers that let you sort bills by the day of month they are due: a bill comes in, you glance at it, and stick it in its appropriate spot. Bill organizers also come in wall models. Or, if you can't stand having your bills staring you in the face, you can organize them in a file drawer or desk drawer.

The Work-from-Home Home Office

This is a very different animal from the occasional office. This room needs to be comfortable and conducive to work. The distractions possible when working at home are many, so the office needs to keep you at your desk.

◄ If clients or other visitors will be visiting your home office, you will need to provide comfort- able seating for them.

Office decorating is more focused around function than fashion. Your office should certainly have an overall decorating style, but function should always win out over décor in this room. That doesn't mean things will clash in style. It just means, for instance, that when you find that perfect oak country-style table that you would love to have as a desk area, you should also remember that if you plan to put your computer on it, your keyboard will be too high. You can get creative and find a keyboard holder to screw underneath the table. Or you can set the table up as a desk and put your computer on a computer stand perpendicular to it—if the computer stand is simple and black, it will hardly stand out, and you can maintain your décor.

This office will also need lots more furnishings than just the desk. Don't forget stands and cabinets for fax machines, phone equipment, surface space for spreading out projects, file storage, book storage, paper storage—the list is nearly endless.

Decorate this room sparingly. Don't include a pile of stuffed animals or a collection of model trains. Unless the room is huge, this is too much. If these collections are your pride and joy and they make you happy when you look at them, choose a favorite and give it a place of honor in your office. Or rotate different pieces from your collection. But unless the collection is containable and easily displayed—a group of signed golf balls or blue ribbons from horse shows—the best rule is to display the collection as a whole somewhere else in the house.

Carpets should be sedate and not distract you from the work at hand. Large, dramatic artwork in an office building is one thing; in your home office, it may be a bit much unless the room you are working with is particularly large.

ALERT!

If you need to use metal furnishings in your home office, many of them can be painted to blend in better with the surroundings. Black always blends well unless your décor is extremely light. White metal can be almost unnoticeable in a room with bright white woodwork.

The Guest Room

Being able to set aside a room just for visitors to sleep in is a luxury indeed. Most people will probably want this room to be dual-purpose. When you have no guests, perhaps this room makes a nice hideout for quiet reading. Choose simple décor, and have a foldout bed, such as a futon for more contemporary décor or a sleep sofa in your chosen decorating style. Then you can offer a comfortable bed for your guests but leave space to use the room for other purposes—spreading out a craft project, exercising, ironing—for every day.

Be sure to include a place for a guest to set a suitcase. You don't want the room to resemble a hotel room, but an old piano bench, a small, freshly painted garden bench, or an old wrought-iron treadle sewing machine stand with a new top will work fine.

The guest room in your home can either carry through the decorating style of the rest of the house or, since this room is used less often and tends to be a bit out of the way anyway, you might rather have fun with a decorating style that is completely different from the rest of your home. Guest rooms can be a great place to put decorations and furniture that you no longer need or want to use in other rooms in the house. Imagine a room that looks like a rural retreat in your midtown rowhouse or a completely contempo room in your otherwise Victorian setting. No one says you can't!

FACT

Make guest rooms easy to clean. After guests leave, simply strip sheets, fold up the sofa bed or futon, replace cushions or slip-cover, and move the coffee table back that did double duty as a suitcase stand.

Decorate the walls with family portraits and photos of family members engaged in sports and hobbies so your guests can enjoy getting a glimpse of your lives at their leisure without having to sit through a slide show. If you have guests who come once a year, use simple frames and change the photos to reflect your family's year.

The Mudroom

In a home where outdoor work is common, a mudroom is not a luxury—it's a necessity. But it also doesn't have to be just a pile of dirty boots and wet gloves. If things have a place to go, they are more likely to be put away, and this room can be kept organized.

Hang strips of pegs wherever you can. Peg strips don't necessarily have to create a country or Shaker look—if your home décor is very modern, paint them black with yellow triangle shapes or follow a Victorian instinct and paint them deep red and add some decorative fringe along the bottom. Rain gear, overshirts, jackets, and hats need a place to go.

Likewise for shoes. Imelda Marcos jokes aside, we all collect shoes for all occasions—boots for mud, boots for warmth, sneakers for walking, running, or style (like those red high-tops), clogs for casual wear. This room will house many shoes despite the collection of dressy shoes in each family member's personal clothes closet.

Look in Spiegel's and other home decorating products catalogs to find things like electric boot dryers and towel racks that can make the mudroom even more functional. Use plastic bins that you can see through, or mark bins with their contents and store seasonal items like wool mittens and heavy gloves or bright orange hats and vests for woods walking during hunting season. These plastic storage bins come in an array of colors and can easily become part of the décor.

QUESTION?

Do I have to be true to a decorating style in all rooms?
When it comes to the less significant rooms in your home, it is best to stretch your decorating style to meet the needs of the room. While you may not want to go postmodern in an otherwise country-style home, it may also be a bit refreshing to have a room or two with an attitude all their own. But the less prominent rooms in a house often have very specific functions, and those functions should be your top consideration.

Don't forget two important things:

- *Lighting:* This area should be able to be brightly lit so you can see to untie shoelaces, find a dropped mitten, or button coats.
- *Seating:* The best seat for the mudroom is a bench with a hinged lid where you can store things. If the bench seat has a back, you can get even more storage space out of it by adding coat hooks on either side.

Some sort of carpeting is probably going to be necessary. This is where you are smart to abandon style considerations and simply choose the best-looking indoor/outdoor carpeting you can find. Scatter rugs are nice because they can be easily taken outside and shaken, but they can get messy pretty quickly in this room that lends itself to clutter anyway.

The Laundry Room

The washer and dryer are the king and queen of the laundry room. Everything else works around them. Shelving over the washer and dryer is great, but unless everyone in your family is six feet tall, only store things up there that won't be used very often. If the room is spacious, a folding table, an ironing board, and laundry baskets are all the most important decorating items you could add. Hang a nice photo or print or dried flower arrangement in an empty space on the wall, and call it a day for decorating this super-functional room.

If you need to pass through the laundry room regularly, either install doors in front of shelves or use unusual furniture like bureaus and hutches to allow laundry paraphernalia to be hidden behind closed doors.

The Library

A library's primary purpose is to house the family's book collection. The library's two most important decorating considerations are storage and comfort.

To serve that purpose, the first thing you need to think about are bookcases. If you have built-in bookshelves, the thinking is done for you already. Maybe you have one wall of built-in bookcases, but that won't be enough for all the books you plan to put in the room. Either install more built-ins, shop for standing bookcases that can mesh with the built-ins already in place, or look in secondhand stores for a mishmash of interesting bookcases to round out the rest of the room.

If the library room isn't big enough for all your books, you can look for some effective ways of making space. What kinds of books do you most look at in your library? Is this room a place where you read for pleasure? If so, plan to put books there that you are inclined to pick up when you sit down to relax. Avid bookbuyers often buy books that they don't read for years—keep these in the library. Also good for the library are collections of essays, short fiction, poetry, and serious nonfiction—the kinds of books you often don't pick up and read from cover to cover.

Other books can find a place elsewhere in the house—cookbooks on a shelf in the kitchen; gardening books in the living room (where they can even be decorative); business and personal finance books in the home office; and novels you have read but want to keep in a lovely bookcase in a guest room.

Furnishing the Library

If the library is to be used for serious study or research, a table of some size is important. A long, narrow library table, like the kind found in a real library, makes a perfect piece. Some sort of table, round or rectangular, is helpful when you need a place to spread out your books.

If you have the space, include a comfortable chair or two, accompanied by an end table and perhaps a coffee table or an ottoman for each chair. Libraries are often places for naps, too, so if you can exchange one of the chairs for a loveseat, that is quite nice. However, you don't want to make the room so comfortable that users automatically fall asleep as soon as they sit down.

Flooring

Wall-to-wall carpeting is all you need, even better if it already exists in the library. It is warm and quiet. Wood flooring is a fine addition to this room that is rich with leather and bound books, and handsomely decorated carpets in deep reds and greens are appropriate choices. If you've chosen to decorate your library more boldly and have created a modern look with metal shelving and a glass-top table, then dress the floor accordingly with a large area rug with bold geometric designs.

◀ A comfortable chair and small table placed near the book shelves in the library will invite people to sit down for a while with a book or two.

Brown is a good color for a library, to promote quiet serious study. However, if your library is used for not-so-serious work, lighter, relaxing shades of green or blue work well.

Good Task Lighting

As the library is by definition a place to read, lighting is obviously a key consideration in this room. Be sure that every sitting place, including the library table, has a good lamp to accompany it. Halogen lamps that can be dimmed or brightened to different intensities make great choices for a library that is used in different ways. If you have substantial built-in bookcases, or whatever you use for shelving your books, find a way to light them up. Individual lighting for each shelf may be too much, but you can do a lot with clamp-style desk lamps. Overhead lighting is not specifically necessary, but it's always a good thing to have in any room for cleaning and for the possibility that the room might someday be transformed for a different use.

Artwork and Accessories

The library is a great place to display artwork. Shelving is obviously the prime consideration, but if the room is big enough and you can afford the wall space, a fine painting in keeping with the style you've chosen for the room makes a great relief from all the shelves and books. If wall space is at a premium, consider a sculpture that can go on a table or on a pedestal.

Check out the unique offerings from Levenger's, a company that offers "tools for serious readers." This company has things like globes, lap desks, wheeled bookshelves, unusual lights, and other useful and attractive items that are right at home in your library and elsewhere in the house. Their Web site is ✍ *www.levenger.com* and their toll-free number for credit card orders is ✆ (800) 544-0880.

Find a separate unit with a glass door to showcase a fine antiquarian book collection. This keeps old books in good shape and dust free. And if the books are not of the sort to be picked up and looked through, get a unit with a locking door and stash the key.

Keep the knickknacks to an absolute minimum in the library. Books collect enough dust that you will want to dust this room frequently, so don't add to the task with lots of little items. Again, if you insist on some collectible collection in the library—letter openers, fine pens, or inkwells would certainly be appropriate—put it behind glass. A collection of bookmarks would look great in a large frame hanging on the wall or secured to the door.

Mirrors are nice in the library, helping add to the idea of an expanse of books. A sizeable clock in your chosen decorating style goes well in this room as well. If you use the library as a retreat and would rather not have the time staring you down from a large clock face, find a couple of small interesting clocks and hide them on a couple of bookshelves so you can peek at the time if you want. Ⓔ

Chapter 19
Outdoor Rooms

Who doesn't want to bring the outdoors into their homes? The porch, deck, gazebo, garden room, sunroom, balcony, and screen house all accomplish that. Decorating these outdoor spaces requires different considerations than other rooms, but the job opens up many fun possibilities, too.

The Possibilities

If your home was built in the latter half of the twentieth century, you may have a deck that was built with the original house. Even homes from earlier eras are likely to have had a deck added on at some point.

Gazebos have become quite popular over the years. With the ease of kits and ready-built models that can be delivered to your home in one piece, they are common sights as you drive the countryside. Gazebos and decks have even often become married together, with a deck sporting a gazebo on its outer edge.

The open front porch has been with us for a while. In the United States, this transitional room that takes you from the rustic outdoors to the more polished indoors came to the height of popularity in the late 1800s and really has never looked back.

Because they are often transitional spaces and by nature are very exposed to the elements, cleaning is a main consideration in your outdoor room décor. However, this doesn't mean that you are stuck with pipe-molded furniture that you cover with plastic the minute you go inside. Lots of contemporary materials hold up well to rain and sun and can be hosed down to wash off the dust and pollen. But the most classic of all materials—wood—still remains a great choice for outdoor room furnishings.

E ALERT!

Don't use propane camping lanterns in an outdoor room that is mostly enclosed. They are appropriate only for spaces that are well ventilated.

Think of your outdoor space like any other space in your house. Don't leave it as a decorating afterthought—in fact, the front porch to your home is the first thing guests—and you!—see, so it should represent the overall feel of your home and make your guests feel welcome. It is rare that a porch commonly covered in dirt and stacked with old junk and out-of-season paraphernalia, like skis in summer and fly-fishing equipment in January, opens up into an elegantly appointed entryway and home decorated to perfection. Your porch will reveal a lot about your house.

But even if you are decorating a deck off the back of the house that few people will ever see, take the design style from your home's interior and carry it out to your outdoor rooms.

Furnishing Outdoor Spaces

Furnishing the outdoor room doesn't have to be challenging. The key is comfort—chances are if you have a gazebo or porch, you go there to relax. Pick comfortable, easy-to-clean furniture.

Withstanding the Elements

Just because you want the furniture to be easy to clean doesn't mean you have to sit on hard plastic. Don't go for plastic cushions that on a hot summer day make you put down a towel to keep the backs of your thighs from sticking to the chair. What's the point in that? Use cushions with cloth covers that are easy to slip off and stick in the wash. Cushion covers are easy to make and can easily match your other porch décor.

Chairs are a main concern for furnishing a porch, patio, or deck, preceded in importance only by a table. A folding wood table, a table with a ceramic tile surface, even a concrete table for a more rustic patio (you don't want to have to move this!) are all fun pieces of outdoor furniture to look for.

ESSENTIAL

Aluminum is a great material for outdoor furniture. It is rustproof, lightweight, and often compact, making it easier to move and easy to store. And it doesn't have to be just silver—the aluminum tubing of chairs and chaise lounges can come in brilliant colors.

If the table isn't going to be out in the weather, you will have a more stylish range of tables to consider. For tables that are going to have to hold up to the elements—sun, rain, and even snow—you will probably want to avoid wood and go for glass, rustproof metal, or even plastic. Plastic is not as pleasing as more natural materials, but on the plus side, a plastic table is easy to clean.

Useful Additions

Make your outdoor room an easy place to eat a meal if that's what you like to do there. If you have room, put a piece of furniture on the porch that has drawers to hold silverware and table linens, salt and pepper, and a candlestick or two. Then you don't have to run in and out of the house with all this stuff each time you eat dinner, which can be somewhat frustrating. If the porch is too small for that kind of thing, keep a tray handy that can carry all the necessary items in one trip.

◀ An enclosed sunroom is a nice option for an outdoor room that will still protect you from the elements and is enjoyable year-round.

Or put a picnic basket under the table and keep all these items stored in the basket—who says you have to go somewhere and sit on the grass to have a picnic! Don't use the oldest, dingiest linens you have just because you're outside. You can still enjoy matching linens and tablecloth outside. An outdoor setting with trees and plants and wood furniture turn quite elegant with a couple of candlesticks and a vase of cut flowers on a white damask tablecloth.

A deck or patio can get an immediately festive look with an umbrella table, also a useful and practical item. If you don't want the umbrella to dominate the color choice for your outdoor space, get one that is neutral in color—beige, white, black, or even dark blue or dark green can highlight rather than overwhelm other color schemes.

A trunk or bench with a hinged seat makes a nice place to stash some games for evening entertainment. They can also be used to store a couple of throw blankets for when the evening turns cool.

The Ultimate Outdoor Furnishing—The Hot Tub

Hot tubs are not only great things to have around, but they can be beautiful, too. One that is surrounded by wood is a rich focal point for any outdoor room. They aren't terribly expensive to run, are less complicated than swimming pools to keep clean, and their health benefits make them well worthwhile.

FACT

Wicker is often thought of as an outdoor furniture style, yet it is not necessarily waterproof. Be sure you paint unfinished wicker with a waterproof paint before leaving it in an outside room. If your wicker furniture is older, repaint it with waterproof paint. Although real wicker is always more inviting, there are some good plastic imitations out there if you don't want the bother of painting. As far as bother goes, however, keep in mind that painting furnishings can be a lot of work, but as a bonus you get to match them exactly as you want to your decorating scheme.

Plants

Plants are a natural for outdoor rooms. A gazebo or porch can provide just the right amount of sun for plants. If you hang plants on an open deck, be sure to pick plants that can stand the full sunlight and potential water they will get from being out all the time. You don't want to have to go to the trouble of bringing plants in and out all the time. They need to be secured to hold up to the wind, especially if they could swing or fall and hit someone on the head! Lastly, if you live in a cold climate and you choose to put houseplants on the deck, in the gazebo, or on the porch, make sure you have enough room for them in the house in the winter months.

Lighting Your Outdoor Space

As when you choose the lighting for any room, you need to be clear about what types of things you will use your outdoor room for. Is it a place where people go to relax and read? A reading lamp for each chair will be necessary. For outdoor decorating, you want the lamps to be outdoor safe and in outdoor style. Unless your porch is fairly enclosed, almost another room in the house, don't decorate with indoor things like lamps with heavy velvet-and-fringe shades. These will just become dirty and aren't designed to get wet, which can happen in any outdoor room if the wind is blowing the rain just right. Besides, if you live in a northern climate, you don't want to have to strip the room every year of all its furnishings and bring them in for the winter, requiring yet another storage space.

When you give your outdoor room a spring cleaning, consider changing the decorations at the same time so the room gets a fresh look every year.

Many outdoor lighting fixtures are stylish and can be bought at your local home improvement store. If the gazebo is away from the house and is wired for electricity, you can use plug-in fixtures that you can move around if you want to. Battery-operated lights can provide enough light for reading although the batteries often don't last long. Solar-powered lights are very popular. They are used mostly for illuminating pathways and for ambient light and aren't as appropriate for task lighting.

Consider fun lighting for your outdoor room, like those decorative strings of horse lights or Japanese lanterns. Even if you aren't actually in the gazebo or screen porch, these lights can make it fun to look at in the evening after dark!

Flooring Considerations

Wood is a common material of porch floors. On a porch that is enclosed, or mostly enclosed, you can even use rugs of almost any style. You won't want to put an antique Persian carpet out there, but almost anything other than an antique will be fine for a porch that is protected from the elements.

Painted wood floors are very porch-style. They can be any color, although a light gray, white, or light blue are nice choices to lighten up an outdoor room.

Pressure-treated wood has become controversial over the past few years. The most common process for treating the wood so that it holds up to moisture and insect damage involves the use of arsenic. This has caused some concern that the arsenic leaches into the soil and can cause environmental problems, particularly contamination of groundwater supplies. Some wood treated with things other than arsenic are coming onto the market. Be sure to keep these concerns in mind when selecting wood.

Porches or patios that are on the ground level may have stone, slate, or even "Florida tile" floors. Tile in the Southwestern style is quite common. It depends on how they are pieced together as to how much you can do with rugs and softening up the flooring. These materials are very rich looking and are great for enhancing the outdoor feel.

There is, of course, always the old standby: fake grass. If you have a patio or porch where you want carpet, but it gets so dirty that you throw it away each year, fake grass carpeting may be the way to go. Unfortunately, this material is an unnatural green in color and is not very comfortable under the feet.

Cleaning Concerns

An area intended for relaxation can be a pretty quick turnoff when it is dirty and dusty. If you live in a northern climate, plan to conduct a springtime porch cleaning each year after the porch has spent the winter being used as just a passageway. A gazebo or screen house will beg for a good cleaning each spring also when it is opened up for the season. Even the deck that gets a constant rinsing from the open elements will benefit from a concentrated wash-down with Murphy's Oil Soap and warm water. You don't need to do this more than once a year.

◄ This bathroom includes doors that open to a private deck outside.

Include all the furnishings in your cleaning as well. White summer-time clothes can be quickly soiled if you sit on moldy or dusty furnishings. And if you use your porch or deck for afternoon tea, you'll want the space to be light and fresh anyway.

Clean the sitting surfaces as well as the floor, the walls, and the ceiling of any outdoor room. Brush cobwebs out and plug up holes where insects and rodents can easily get in and illicitly enjoy the room at your expense. If your outdoor setting enables you to decorate with wallhangings or other decorative items, give them a good scrubbing as well.

Accessories

Purchasing wind chimes can be a big decision! Quality crafts stores that sell handmade chimes often have a display that lets you to listen to how each wind chime sounds. Picking one out that suits your and your housemates' ears can be a difficult job. However, these decorations are beautiful for outdoor rooms. While their aural as well as visual beauty is part of their charm, if you hang them in a somewhat protected spot, they won't chime with every little wisp of a breeze. If you have close neighbors, they will appreciate that as well.

FACT

The term "veranda" hails from India, where this open porch style abounds.

If you don't want to listen to chimes at all but want something fun to hang from the ceiling of the porch or balcony, have some fun making a mobile out of some appropriate things like seashells or pine cones.

Birdfeeders are often a fun thing to hang from the deck or near an outdoor room of any kind. However, don't forget that where there are birds, there are also bird droppings. And there are also likely to be squirrels, chipmunks, mice, and other rodents that enjoy snacking on the birdseed. You may not want to encourage these critters to come up onto your deck. Instead, you may be better off putting your birdfeeders away from the house, where you can view the birds while sitting outside on the deck.

You can even stick to a Victorian decorating theme with your outdoor room décor. Hang a birdcage with a plant in it, some heavily flowered houseplants, dark linens, floral prints on the chairs, and combined with some gingerbread trim on the screen door or braces of the gazebo and *voilà!* you are as Victorian outside as in.

How do I stop the dog from popping out the screen door?
Exuberant dogs don't understand the concept of screens. It does get tiresome repairing a screen time and time again, and if you live in a climate where bugs rule the world, you don't want those screens open very long. Next time you find yourself ready to replace a screen, ask your local repair shop about pet-strength screening. This heavier duty screening is designed to discourage dogs. However, its strength means a little less air flow and slightly reduced clarity when it comes to visibility.

Feng Shui Outside

Good feng shui by its very nature is influenced by the outdoors. Everything about feng shui is directed by compass points and elements in nature. Don't forget to encourage good energy flow and an inviting atmosphere in an outdoor room. Here are some things to consider.

Does your porch give the visitor a welcome feeling? Is it neat and orderly, and does it not make you want to rush into the house to get beyond the mess and clutter? Clear the room out and, if clutter tends to accumulate, add some storage and organizing furniture to give things a place to go. In summer, keep a vase on a table or stand and let some fresh flowers brighten your entry.

Does your home have a view of water of some kind? A pond, a brook, even a fountain perhaps? By all means focus the outdoor room's attention around it. Water is a very auspicious element to good feng shui as long as it does not hurry through the property but lingers a bit while passing through. Focus on water and natural elements like trees and rocks where possible.

If your outdoor space isn't placed near water, bring water to it. Fountains are easy to come by these days and are mostly simple to construct. Place the structure where you want it, attach a hose, plug in an electric pump to keep the water circulating, and you have a creek. Or construct a small pond and stock it with fish. Any chance you might be able to put a Plexiglass viewing area on the floor and let the fish swim under the gazebo or deck? That's always a great focal point for any outdoor room!

Lighting is critical to good feng shui. A deck or gazebo in the backyard may be more inclined toward subtle, even romantic lighting, but you want to have plenty of lighting for the use of the room. Obviously, a greenhouse or conservatory needs and is designed to get a lot of natural light. Depending on where it is placed on the property, a gazebo gets lots of natural light in the daytime but also does well to be appropriately lit at night. If you never eat dinner in the gazebo (what a shame!) maybe some low lighting is enough, but if you eat, read, knit, whittle, or whatever in this outdoor room, be sure you give yourself the appropriate light.

Chapter 20

Antiques, Secondhand Items, and Flea Market Fare

Decorating your home with antiques is a fun way to give your home a unique flair. Antiques never go out of style, and they can fit into just about any decorating style. If you decide to collect even just a piece or two, there are a lot of things to learn and know about antique collecting and decorating with your finds.

Getting Started with Antiques

If you have never collected antiques before, you will be quickly overwhelmed with the sheer number of things that are available to collect. Perhaps the best place to begin is with something you need—maybe you can decide to collect one piece a year or every other year, or one piece per room, or in some other organized fashion that allows you to organize your search. That something may be a large piece of furniture like a hutch, but it could also be a collection of small items to fill a glass-fronted shelving nook in the dining room or just a fun decorative item like a carousel horse.

The number of places to shop for antiques is quite mindboggling. Almost any town in America has classic antique shops. And then, of course, there are many shops that call themselves "antique" shops but that sell mostly used items that are not antiques at all. If you know what you are looking for, these shops can contain some gems hidden in nooks and crannies. If you are new to the antiquing business and definitely want an antique, stick to the reputable shops.

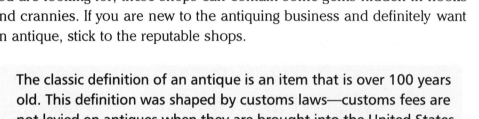

FACT

The classic definition of an antique is an item that is over 100 years old. This definition was shaped by customs laws—customs fees are not levied on antiques when they are brought into the United States (as long as they are not intended for resale). Therefore a concrete measure of what constituted an "antique" was established.

If you can't afford antiques or are concerned you won't use a piece once you buy it, consider reproductions. Quality reproductions are still expensive, but they have the potential of becoming antiques themselves. And if reproductions are over one hundred years old, you still have an antique, and perhaps a valuable one, on your hands.

Antiques Research

Information is the key to successful antique buying. The more you know about a piece, the better you'll be able to understand whether it is really worth the price or worth passing up. The Internet has become the antique lover's savior. There are hundreds of sites to search, and those sites all have several links to lesser known sites. You can sit in your home and shop on the famous Portobello Road in London or even the infamous antique auction houses like Sotheby's in New York.

Appraisals

Many of these Web sites also offer appraisal services. For a fee, you can fax, send, or e-mail them a picture of an item that you own and want to know more about (or one you're considering purchasing). The more detail the picture shows, the better. Describe the specifics of the piece, such as any cracks, nicks, blemishes, signatures, dates, and so on. The appraiser will ask other specific questions based on information that is known about the piece, and you will get an appraisal of what the piece may be worth.

If a shop owner will let you take a photo of the piece, that's great. Digital cameras can be perfect for this purpose. Sometimes dealers have photos they've already taken. Many shop owners will document for you the research they did to decide on a price for a piece.

Beyond the appraisal price, there is the emotional factor to consider. Is this a piece that would enhance your decorating scheme perfectly? Then it may be worth a little more to you, or at least worth the asking price. On the other hand, if you don't care if a piece slips through your hands, negotiate vigorously!

You will gradually gain experience that will help you decide some things yourself. However, if you are considering a large outlay for an antique piece, by all means get an appraisal from an uninvolved party.

A reputable antique dealer will have an idea of the price range that a piece can command. However, there are many variables that make an antique worth more or worth less, and sometimes substantially more or less, and as a buyer, you will want some help. You can either look in your yellow pages for a local appraiser, have pieces appraised online at some of the reputable online antique sites, or get a referral from someone you know who collects.

Like any professional you hire, make sure this person has credentials and can refer you to former clients. The local antiques dealers should recognize the appraiser at least by reputation—the antiques market is huge, but like every other industry it becomes pretty small once you get involved and realize that everybody knows everybody!

Antique Dictionary

You certainly could collect antique dictionaries. To give you a head start, here are just a few terms you will run across time and time again if you get into looking at antiques.

As Is

Anyone who has bought or sold something along the side of the driveway—a bicycle, a car—is familiar with the phrase "as is." With simple secondhand things, this mostly means that the seller does not guarantee the condition of the item as being perfect and that whatever is wrong with it becomes the responsibility of the buyer, not the owner.

In the antiques market, the phrase "as is" is more likely to mean that there is actually some blemish that makes it less valuable. This may make the price more appealing, which may be exactly what you want if the item is one you simply want to have. But if it is an antique you are purchasing for its value and for potential resale, the blemish will hurt the resale value as well. The decision of whether it's still worth buying is yours to make. It depends a lot on what the piece is and what the blemish is.

Daguerreotype

This refers both to a photograph done in a particular way and the process of creating that photograph. A daguerreotype photo is produced on a silver or a silver-colored copper plate. Age is easy to establish with these antiques, since the process was among the earliest type of photo processing in the middle of the nineteenth century.

Ephemera

The word ephemera has become somewhat synonymous with collectibles. It has also come to be used for secondhand shops signs or names, lending a little higher brow to the items sold within than the ordinary term "secondhand." Ephemera refers to collectible objects, like posters, that were not intended to be long-lived and therefore have no lasting value and, therefore, are not antiques.

Memorabilia

The dictionary definition of memorabilia is "things that stir recollection." They can be antiques or not, depending on the item. For instance, Pez candy dispensers would be memorabilia for baby boomers who recall them from their childhood (although they have never really stopped being available).

Patina

A patina refers to the coating an item acquires with age (especially things made of wood or metals), a natural coating from oxidation, dirt, and from handling. This "patina" is actually a good thing when it comes to antiques. Keeping the patina is one of the reasons that you should never refinish an antique unless you don't care if it loses some value.

Reproduction

A reproduction doesn't only refer to knockoffs that are less expensive than the real thing. A reproduction of an original design can be an antique itself, depending on when the reproduction was done and by whom.

FACT

Many Web sites are available to help with antique purchase and appraisal. Check out ✍ www.antiques.org for a Web ring of antiques dealers. On the site ✍ www.tias.com dealers sell thousands of antiques and collectibles. This site is host to the king and queen of antiques, Terry and Ralph Kovel. Their antique guides are classics themselves, and their Web site includes a newsletter full of information for collectors as well as an appraisal service and other great links.

Vernacular

Webster's defines "vernacular" as "of, relating to, or characteristic of a period, place, or group." This characteristic of furniture design helps place a piece in history and helps to value it as an antique.

Caring for Antiques

Be prepared to take good care of your antiques. Find out the exact best way to clean them. Set them in places that keep them away from things that can damage them. For instance, an antique quilt will not last long if hung in a room that gets bright sunlight most of the day. But remember, antiques have held up for a long time already, so don't be afraid to buy old things with the intention of using them. If you do plan to use an antique item on a daily basis, buy for quality of craftsmanship, not just design.

If you like antiques, you'll love the popular PBS series *Antiques Roadshow* which has been running since 1996. The show tours the country appraising antiques brought in by local people. The show and its Web site are must-sees. The site contains the schedule for their summer road trips and has unique information about antiques and the people who collect them, like the man who is specifically interested in topographical errors. And don't miss their "resources" button: this is a complete list of the 300 reference works that travel with them. This is quite a list and alone worth a visit to the site. The address is *www.pbs.org/wgbh/pages/roadshow/.*

Antiques as Decoration

Some antique items make perfect decoration. Tools are a great example. Before the mass production processes that we have today, tools were made of the finest woods and metals. They included little details to give them a touch of distinction courtesy of the craftsman who made them. Look at an old handsaw, and you will find a rich wood handle with some decorative carving and a carefully designed handgrip that has a little more flair than is technically necessary. Today's everyday tools tend to be very utilitarian without the embellishments that make older tools a joy to look at. Without overdoing it, a few tools hung carefully on the walls can make the perfect decorating items for an office, entryway, or porch.

Other antiques that are commonly collected and used for decoration are glass, porcelain, and crockery, prints, maps, books, and old bottles.

Decorative Techniques

Several basic types of decorative techniques were used on early pieces. You may find them in your search for antique items. Here is a little more information on the most popular:

- *Country painting:* This simple style of decorative painting was often done on tinware and common in the mid-1700s.
- *Freehand bronze:* A bronze powder is applied over a partially dry base coat of paint. This technique is commonly found in eighteenth-century pieces.
- *Stenciling:* Stenciling consists of cutting out a stencil and applying paint to create a somewhat elaborate decoration that can be repeated exactly. This technique was developed in the early nineteenth century and is still popular today.
- *Floating color:* A painting technique in which colors are floated on a varnish and linseed oil mixture. This technique requires some skill.
- *Gold leaf:* Again, a skilled art in which thin sheets of gold are applied to a coat of paint. This technique is very decorative and was used in early eighteenth-century England and in the United States shortly after.
- *Distressing:* There are many techniques for making an item look antique, including roughing it up with a wire brush, carefully scorching it, or staining it with tea.

Tomorrow's Antiques

Don't forget when you are buying new items to buy good quality things that will wear well and last over time. The amazing rate at which we dispose of plastic, our cheaply made appliances that break down or wear out so quickly, compared to the heavy duty appliances of old, are just more signs of how we buy for the moment. It's easier to throw out a toaster than repair it, and, in fact, many appliances these days cannot be repaired at all.

▲ Real antiques can be matched with newer pieces that have an old-fashioned look to them.

Think about collecting the antiques of tomorrow. Perhaps these are secondhand items that do not yet quite meet the century-old requirement. Or perhaps they are custom-made items that will be around 100 years from now. Custom made does not have to mean one-of-a-kind, which is costlier. Custom simply means an item is not factory made in mass production but rather made one at a time for your order. You can probably request some specific changes. Be prepared to place a decent deposit and to wait three to five months for your item, so plan ahead if you are redecorating a room and want to order a specific custom piece. The wait is worth it for an item that may well become a family heirloom.

Secondhand Shop and Flea Market Savvy

Don't stuff your home so full of collections from secondhand shops that your home could itself be a shop. A way to get around this is to go shopping with a list of items you are looking for: blue glassware, a plate for the third rung of your new wrought-iron plate holder, a stool to paint to match the red accents in your kitchen. Sometimes it's fun to just go see what you find, but a lot of times it is just too overwhelming. You can easily spend all day shopping and still come home without the item you were hoping for, or you can end up buying things you don't really need or want.

Don't get too specific in your list, however; it's almost impossible to find exactly what you want. It is easier, for example, to find a ten-gallon crock with a design on the front than to find a ten-gallon crock with a bird design on the front. The bird designs are certainly out there, but if you're searching for something that specific, you will probably have better luck searching online at the larger antique sites.

ALERT!

Repair work on authentic antique pieces does devalue the piece. Sometimes the repair is necessary. If the piece is rare enough, the value will probably still be high. A known repair is not a reason to absolutely not buy a piece, but be aware of the negative impact of repairs on the value of antique pieces.

Don't be afraid to offer a lower price on significant items. Whenever you enter into a negotiation, however, you should be prepared both to walk away and to pay something more than your lowest offer.

Secondhand Stuff That You Already Own

Think out of the box when it comes to incorporating your finds into your home. Not only is it nice to find some whimsical items, it's also fun to find things that you can reuse in a new way. In other words, give things a new life with a new purpose. Some ideas include the following:

- Buckets and watering cans become flower pots, either for cut flowers or plantings. If the bottom of a watering can is rusted, you can cut it out and plant something in it and let the roots go right into the earth from there.
- Windows don't have to remain windows, especially if they have interesting frames. Replace the glass with mirrored glass, and you have an interesting mirror that can give a landlocked room a false sense of the outdoors.
- Old egg-collecting baskets make great collectors for the vegetable garden.

Organize Your Shopping

Secondhand-store shopping should mean lots of fun, not lots of headache. The best way to find great items at secondhand stores is to visit those stores often. Secondhand shops get new items on a regular basis. These may be just the things you're looking for! If you visit a shop often, the owner will get to know your tastes and interests and will call you when things come in that you might be interested in.

If that's not serendipitous enough for your flea-market shopping tastes, then pick a few shops that you visit regularly. If you don't have a lot of time to linger, you will quickly be forced to become an expert at assessing the possibilities of flea-market items.

Determine what you would be willing to spend on something, and don't be afraid to ask the shopowner if he or she will take your lower offer. Unless it's an item you really want—the matching bowl to a nesting set whose third-smallest bowl you broke—then you can always walk away. If you are truly a flea-market shopper, the next item you get interested in will be as exciting as the one that got away. Ⓔ

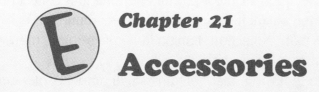

Chapter 21

Accessories

Small details can make or break your style. They can affect the feeling of a room in subtle ways. Don't forget whimsy. Fun is a great part of accessorizing—be sure to include some things around your home that make you smile when you see them and provide guests with a touch of surprise. Use common things in uncommon ways. In other words, have fun with decorating!

The Basics

Every accessory decorating your home doesn't need to exactly balance. Sometimes being off balance is balance, and sometimes too much balance is boring. Put things where they are pleasing to the eye. If you aren't sure, enlist the help of a family member or friend. You'll won't ever go wrong by using the largest or most prominent thing in a collection as the focal point and then balancing your other pieces around it. For instance, to display a plate collection, hang a large platter first, then work the other smaller dishes in around it.

If there is a fabric in a room that contains small amounts of a certain bold color, you can help that color pop out of the fabric more by adding a small bit of the color somewhere nearby. A piece of pottery or some candlesticks in the same color can draw that color out of the fabric.

Too much is just too much. You know what it's like to walk into a secondhand shop or a huge department store and be so overwhelmed with stuff you don't know what to look at first. Don't make your home look like a secondhand shop. Leave the crowds of stuff to the flea market. That doesn't mean that every accessory needs its own little pedestal with a spotlight, either. Just make sure that the things you choose to put in your home hold some sort of meaning. Things passed down from members of the family are always meaningful, as are items you buy while traveling. Combining memories with decoration is an age-old practice.

You can put a lot more than just photographs in frames. Pick interesting frames and hang your favorite poem or letter. If the original piece is too big or too precious, either photocopy it to size or retype it and print it out in some interesting font or color. You can add some decorative motif or illustration or even make a miniature collage. Decorations that hold meaning to a home's occupants are always more special than just any old decoration. For instance, you might frame an old map showing the location of your home.

Accessories for the Walls

There are many items that can grace your walls and provide both style and function at the same time.

Mirrors

Mirrors in the bathroom and dressing area are always functional, but mirrors in other parts of the house can be mostly decorative. One function mirrors serve, as well, is to provide some illusion of a larger space. For feng shui practitioners, mirrors are essential to help disperse energy in blocked areas of the house. You will have no problem finding mirrors with frames in any decorating style you have chosen for your home, from highly ornate gilt-framed mirrors for the Victorian décor to those with black metal for modern styles or wooden frames for the country home.

◀ A mirror in an ornate gold frame accents this living room perfectly.

Wreaths

Wreaths are a classic tradition and no longer relegated to Christmas nor to strictly country décor. Wreaths can be an expression of personal taste and can be a great venue for adding a little whimsy to your home. And the wreath no longer hangs just on the front door, either, although that is still a great place for one. If you want to use items in your wreath that are not weatherproof, hang it in the kitchen, the hall, or the guest bedroom—virtually anywhere in the house. It is also another opportunity to pick up a color hidden in the drapery or upholstery fabric.

Make your wreath look professional by buying a wreath frame in the size you want. From there, create a foundation of something like evergreen boughs, vines, or even fabric that you can then decorate with anything you fancy. Add some ribbon or trim, hang, and enjoy! Like everything else, however, when your wreath begins to look a little weary with dust and cobwebs, take it apart and create a new one. They can be hard to clean, so you may want to plan to replace it regularly, like once a season.

Storage Accessories

What's better than something stylish? Something stylish that also helps you keep clutter under control without getting in the way of your décor. In fact, it even is a *part* of your décor. There are many options for incorporating useful items that will make keeping things neat almost seem fun.

Umbrella Stands

Umbrella stands in the city, where you are likely to do a lot of walking to the corner store, for example, are almost a must. Antique stands can be absolutely beautiful. Even if you don't live in the city, if you have room in your foyer, consider this accessory for a more traditional décor. It can hold other things as well, like walking sticks and canes.

Coat Racks

A coat rack is a convenient item and is available for almost any décor. When you buy a self-standing coat rack, pick a sturdy, well made one that isn't inclined to tip over if it isn't perfectly balanced. Bentwood, Arts & Crafts, and many other styles are readily available. Coat racks can hang on the wall as well; a Shaker peg board is a perfect coat rack in a country-style home.

Magazine Racks

Organization and neatness are key to good decorating. Magazine racks help you get there in a big way. What home doesn't pile up with magazine collections, especially considering how many hobbies and interests have magazines devoted to them? Pick a magazine rack to suit your décor, and use it.

A nice style if you have the space is a tall magazine stand with three or four shelves. The top shelf is usually a little high to serve as an end table—it's too high to set your coffee on while you read—but it makes a great display space for a decorative piece of pottery. The other shelves can hold several magazines each. They allow you to divide magazines up by topic if you like, and they store the magazines flat instead of curling them like a basket on the floor might.

A tiered magazine racks hangs magazines from their spine. They do look nice, but the hanging pages will curl in humidity. Also, they only hold a half dozen or so magazines at a time.

E ALERT!

Think ahead about how you will be able to keep a decorative item clean. For instance, if you put a collection of beach glass in a decorative clear glass container, either choose a container that has a lid to keep dust out or plan to empty the glass pieces out every couple months or so. Rinse the beach glass in warm water, clean the container, carefully dry the glass pieces, and put it back together. Be sure to take the time to do this because dirty decorative items are not decorative at all. Don't choose to decorate with things that you can't or won't keep clean.

Baskets

Baskets can make great storage, but they can also be strictly decorative. People tend to overdo it with baskets. Keep the strictly decorative ones to a minimum, and restrict yourself to displaying uniquely designed or interestingly colored baskets. If you like baskets—and most people think that a country style décor without a basket just isn't country—include them as functional items. Baskets can appear in any room in the house, holding magazines, mittens, or makeup. Use them as organizers, but don't have so many of them that you need something to organize the baskets themselves!

Accents with a Purpose

There are many other accessories that can spruce up your home that also serve very useful purposes.

Footstools

Stools are always a practical item to have in the home. They don't have to be boring, though. Here's where you can experiment with those great paint techniques or try out your skill with decoupage. It is simple to recover small upholstered stools. Your stool can always match your upholstered furniture, or you can use the upholstery to help make one of those accessorizing colors pop out of their hiding places elsewhere in the room.

Quilts

Quilts are beautiful decorative items and are, of course, especially suited to bedrooms. They also can be functional decorations anywhere that an occasional lap blanket or shoulder wrap would be welcome—near a favorite reading chair, for instance.

If you aren't going to keep them spread out on the bed, then consider hanging them on a quilt rack. A rack is only about the size of a standing towel holder—you fold the quilt once or twice and drape it over the top. Some racks have more than one bar. You can either hang multiple quilts or blankets or you can avoid folds in your quilts by hanging one quilt across the top.

Quilts can also be hung on the wall if they are never going to be used. Make sure quilts, especially old ones, aren't hanging in the sun.

Exposure to sunlight will fade their colors and weaken the fabric and threads.

Pottery

Pottery pieces can be the most fun to decorate with. Some pieces of pottery, like pitchers, can also serve as vases to hold cut flower arrangements. Put potpourri in pottery bowls. Use mugs, small pitchers, or colored glass tumblers to hold pens or paper clips on your desk. Decorative dishware and pottery can make everyday needs more pleasing to the eye.

FACT

www.Art.com is a great Web site with thousands of posters, prints, and celebrity photos available for purchase online. The site can be searched by subject or artist and you can have your choice framed before it is shipped.

Fire and Light

The tools that you need for tending a fire in the fireplace or woodstove don't have to be boring. Browse the catalogs, and look for unique items that fit into your home's style. Fireplace tools come in several possible finishes, and their styling has ventured into a wide-ranging arena of designs, from classic to extremely modern. Wood holders can be wrought iron, wooden country-style, or sleek metal. The holders with removable wood totes, such as a fabric sling, are especially useful. Fireplace screens have become an item with many great designs. Since this is a pretty large item in the room, you should shop around to find the one that appeals most to you. Andirons can also round out a style; typically, these items all can be bought as a set in the same style. If you want the fire itself to take center stage, use a simple grate that will be covered up when logs are set on it. Most secondhand or antique stores will have a selection of iron soup pots and other former fireplace necessities.

If you don't use the fireplace for fires, the decorative possibilities for that space are still endless. You could simply set up a fire that never gets lit or decorate with evergreens and other plantings. A fireplace installed with a light can make a great stage for a number of possible scenes that have nothing to do with fireplaces! Or use a grow light and put a couple of plants there. Be prepared to clean this area occasionally, however, since it is at floor level and will get dusty and dirty fast.

Candles

Let's face it, electricity is pretty common in our world. Once an indispensable item in the household, candles are now purely decorative—and lovely decorations at that. No longer restricted to simple, single-color tapers, candles come in any size imaginable. And some of them are works of art. Use candles to enhance a color scheme, even if you never put a match to them. Candle stores can be a bit overwhelming. Either go and buy something that strikes your eye or go with an intention to fill a certain need.

Candleholders

If you buy unusual candles, you may need unusual candleholders to put them in. Use sturdy candleholders that won't tip over easily. Wall sconces are lovely and can be rustic and country or elegant and traditional. Just be sure to use dripless candles in them so the wax doesn't end up on your wall-to-wall carpet.

ALERT!

When cleaning your valued decorative items, use products specifically designed for the material. Employ old soft-bristled toothbrushes to get into crevices, and above all don't clean them too often. No matter how careful you are, cleaning will scratch and rub the finish off any item to at least some degree.

Candleholders can be a lot of fun to choose. Many are inexpensive, and you can find incredibly unusual ones. Candle stores remain popular and offer a fantastic selection. Glass and pottery artisans often create candleholders, so you can get pieces of art that serve a purpose. Candleholders are also common items in most secondhand shops. If you look hard on tables full of stuff, you will find some unusual choices. They make a nice collection to display, or you can tuck them in a closet and pull them out to add pizzazz to your dinner party table.

Other Accessories

The variety of items that you can use to make your house feel like a home is almost endless. Ultimately, almost anything can be decorative—old-fashioned hairbrushes set on a shelf, fancy hair clips or hatpins stuck on a piece of fabric or on a curtain in the bathroom, teacups, golf balls and tees, seashells, interesting hardware, or molds of all kinds that originally were used to make anything from metal to Jell-O.

Clocks

There's nothing quite so majestic in the home as a grandfather clock with a commanding chime. Give it the place of prominence it deserves. Chiming clocks aren't for everyone. However, if you have great patience (or a soundproof room), a cuckoo clock collection can be fun. In a similar vein, clocks are available that strike on the hour with bird sounds, horse sounds, train sounds, or any sound that is appealing to you. A very modern room could have a clock built into the wall itself with a mechanism installed and numbers hand-painted right on the wall. Retro clocks that evoke a fifties or sixties style, with bright plastic flowers or a cat whose tail swings with the seconds, would be great finds in flea markets, yard sales, or secondhand stores. Small clocks that can be tucked onto bookshelves don't need to be completely bland—art galleries can be great places to find little geometric figures or clock faces set into polished beach stones. They aren't terrifically expensive and provide quite a punch for their size—unique yet functional.

Snapshots

We'll talk more about photographs as artwork in Chapter 23. But don't forget snapshots as decorative items. Frames are inexpensive, and shopping for them is a lot of fun. You can either pick them up when you see one you like—on sale or in a secondhand or antique store—and find just the right photo in your collection to put in it. Or you can go shopping for a frame for a special photo that you want to display. If you buy simple frames, it's very easy to switch the photos and almost automatically change your decorating. Scatter them around the house in little nooks and crannies and enjoy decorating your home with your own treasured memories of family vacations, pets, or a close-up of a red tulip in your garden—anything goes!

Plants

Plants are a favorite decorating item. Find the places in your home that are especially suited to plants—sunny windows and steamy bathrooms are a couple of good possibilities. If you are not inclined to be very attentive to your houseplants, pick varieties that don't need a lot of fussing.

African violets are a perennial favorite houseplant. They are not difficult to maintain, and they are easy to cultivate by snipping off a leaf and sticking it in some potting soil until it takes root. African violets come in a wide range of colors, and they are so bold they can be part of the color scheme of any room.

If you want live plants for decoration but aren't inclined to spend a lot of time taking care of them, consider placing them all in one or two areas of the house. That way you can bring a watering can to one spot and water all your plants at once without having to wander throughout the house. Bring along a grocery bag and weed out any dead leaves. If you pick the right plants, you can choose one day of the week to do this and still keep your plants quite happy. Houseplants tend to be overwatered anyway, so one day a week for watering for the hardiest varieties is fine, especially if you avoid hanging them in the hottest south-facing window in the house.

Make Your Own

Accessories can be perfect do-it-yourself craft projects. By making things yourself, you can get exactly what you want in the colors you want. If you don't want to start totally from scratch, there are many places where you can buy unfinished wood items or unpainted greenware and paint them yourself in the design and color to match the room they are intended to go in.

Feng Shui and Accessories

Accessories like mirrors, candles, wind chimes, and crystals can serve both as decorations and as a way to enhance the feng shui in your home. Many decorative items can provide a touch of the color needed to balance the elements in places in your house that need help. For example, if you run a home business, add some purple to the southeast corner—the compass direction controlling wealth—of your home office. Researching feng shui can give you just one more bit of guidance for decorating.

The details of your home are the things that tell a lot about you and that make your home environment intimate and unique. Choose your accessories wisely, and err on the sparse side rather than overdoing it. That way, the precious things that you choose to decorate with will be sure to be seen and not hidden amidst a crowd. (E)

Chapter 22

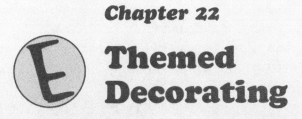

Themed Decorating

Almost no time in the calendar year exists that doesn't allow for some kind of theme that you can use to guide your seasonal home decorating. You can always find a season or holiday to influence your décor. If you're someone who likes to constantly change your decorations, then theme decorating is for you!

Themes You Can Reuse

Redecorating often doesn't have to mean spending lots of money. You can, of course, reuse decorations year after year—make them seem different by using them in a different way or putting them in a different place. Maybe a ribbon color could be changed or the same vase used for elaborate themed arrangements at different times of the year.

Some theme decorations can be a lot of fun—like some of the more expansive Christmas items—so much that you and your neighbors look forward to seeing them each year.

Maybe you could rotate some decorations every year or two so that even you barely remember them the next time you use them. Sell the items you're done with in a yard sale, or donate them to the local Salvation Army for another family to discover and enjoy.

ESSENTIAL

Make use of holiday sales to plan for next year's decorations for any specific holidays. Starting around three days before the holiday and running for maybe a week after, you can find great blow-out sales as stores try to clear the inventory instead of returning it or storing it. Keep things in their original wrappers when you pack them away with the decorations you used this year, and you'll automatically know what is new.

Some holidays hardly need more than a color scheme to evoke the holiday. Decorate in green and red, and you will create an automatic sense of Christmas. Red with touches of white lace can suggest Valentine's Day. Add blue to red and white and you are on your way to patriotic Independence Day decoration. Orange and black have been permanently attached to Halloween, while orange, brown, and perhaps some green can conjure up thoughts of Thanksgiving. All this happens before a heart, flag, or pumpkin have even made an appearance on the scene.

When to Change the Theme

The holidays are, of course, the most obvious time to change decorating themes. The passing of the holiday is a natural point to take the relevant decorations down. How long you like to keep your decorations up before and after the actual holiday is up to you. A good rule of thumb may be two weeks before the holiday and a couple of days after, but if you take your cue from the department stores, you will start to think that Valentine's Day decorating should start the day before Christmas!

A lot will depend on how much the holiday means to you. If you are Irish, you may be much more festive on St. Patrick's Day than your Greek neighbor. Those who really get into Christmas make the holiday a six-week decorating extravaganza, starting before Thanksgiving and leaving decorations up through New Year's. And, hey, if you go to lots of trouble to decorate, why not enjoy it for a while?

But theme decorating doesn't have to revolve just around holidays. Seasonal decorating is a natural—winter, summer, spring, and fall create almost automatic decorating opportunities with a specific beginning and ending. Or perhaps a hobby provides a theme—a love of horses, golf, fishing, or baseball offers endless possibilities for decorating at least one room in the home. These interests probably yield more everlasting decorations that you don't change often.

Collections are another theme to decorate around. Stamp collecting, model trains, dolls, antiques, tools, farm implements, and many other items make perfect topics to focus a decorating scheme. You can have lots of fun creating unusual ways to display and use items that fit your theme. And finding these treasures is just as much fun as using them!

Choosing Themes

Before you decide on a theme, take a look around your home. Themes usually don't need to be sought out, as they often are there already. That's sort of the charm of theme decorating. It's something that's not necessarily planned at first but that just sort of happens, leaving you free later to expand on the idea.

Consider all the same things that you normally consider when you're choosing decorating items to fit into theme topics. If you are not much on dusting, don't make fussy little knickknacks your theme. Or if you insist, then be sure you have a place to put them, like in a glass cabinet, where you can still see the objects but where they won't collect dust.

A house with small children is not the place for a collection of delicate Hummels to be scattered around on end tables and coffee tables. Save yourself and your kids some frustration. Either choose something else to collect, or put those items in the closet or a cabinet with high shelves until the kids are older.

Although a complete diner theme or barn theme can be lots of fun, typically you don't want to try too hard with themes. Some of the best are the themes that are subtle enough that a guest might have to spend a couple of days in your house before starting to pick up the threads that together form your decorating theme.

Theme Means "Many"

If you want a theme for decorating, you will want more than one item or it won't be a theme. If your budget is modest, that means you shouldn't expect antique wood library tables or one-of-a-kind Lalique glass to be your theme.

Look around your home. Chances are you already have the beginning of a theme. Lace doilies that your great grandmother made? Several postcards with birds on them that could be inexpensively framed? A couple of handmade musical instruments that could be displayed and joined with new ones as you find them? Ideas are everywhere. Even books with blue dust jackets, matchboxes, animal skins, art deco posters, or wine bottles can create a theme for you to work within.

The minute family and friends get wind of your theme, you can be sure that the gifts they give you for all your coming days will be dogs, or blue glass, or red-and-white lampshades.

Mini Themes

Themes can come in miniature, too. Stick hatpins through a linen curtain. Collections of glass items—salt and pepper shakers, dog statuettes, goose napkin rings, desk clocks—can constitute theme decorating even if they aren't all showcased together. Scatter them around the house—the bathroom windowsill, the nightstand in the spare bedroom, on top of the television—and enjoy thinking of the smile on a guest's face when he or she begins to put the theme together.

Stretch the Idea

If you want to have an equine theme, think beyond just pictures of horses. Hang tack as decorative items on the walls, and make use of old barn hardware in innovative ways. For example, you could use bits for towel hangers or as curtain tiebacks.

Likewise with other themes—say, race cars. Don't just hang pictures of racing cars on the wall. Use the checkered flag pattern on throw pillow covers, make a clock out of a steering wheel, or hang hubcaps on the wall! Think beyond the obvious when it comes to themes.

Holiday Themes

If you want your holiday decorating to be really fun, try decorating around an unusual holiday in a different country! But if the typical American holidays are enough for you, here are some ideas for the basics.

Christmas

Christmas is by far the most ornately decorated holiday of them all. Whole shops, books, and catalogs are created specifically for Christmas decorations.

FACT

Collected too many ornaments over the years? String them together into a wreath of Christmas bulbs. The wreath can bring back memories of Christmas trees past and leave room on your tree to create new memories.

You can be very traditional with the usual red-and-green combinations and elaborate Victorian styling, or you can stretch the theme to any of your favorite colors and just dress them up accordingly. All-white or all-silver Christmas tree designs are popular offshoots of the standard green tree with colorful bulbs.

A shimmering tablecloth with candles and a garland are elaborate enough without ever having to incorporate any green or red. Besides the obvious religious themes, Christmas has become much more of a simply festive occasion. Use yellows, purples, or deep blues, and add fringe and other decorative elements to create a cozy, warm atmosphere.

Christmas decorating can be practical as well as ornamental. Hang an advent calendar, either handmade or bought, and you get both a useful countdown to Christmas as well as a decorative item. Foodstuffs such as fruit baskets add lovely holiday décor and disappear as the holiday draws near.

Two places that can get lots of attention at Christmas or any holiday are the fireplace mantel and the dining table.

The mantel can serve as a place to hang the traditional Christmas stockings. If you hang a painting or print over your mantel, consider changing it to a piece with a Christmas theme. Trail a real or fake garland across the top of the mantel and intersperse its folds with candles or holiday-related figurines. Hang your favorite tree bulbs from the bottom of the mantel to show them off. The mantel is a very creative space.

The dining table is a must to decorate for the holidays, and Christmas is no exception. Although not completely focused around food as is Thanksgiving, food and gathering for meals are nonetheless very important at Christmas. Decorating the table accordingly is an expected and pleasant thing.

Wreaths are another classic Christmas decoration, although they are not reserved just for Christmas any longer. Make or buy a simple grapevine wreath, and you can change the decorations to match the holiday. To give it a good washing, simply soak the wreath in some water when all decorations are removed. Live wreaths made of evergreens won't last much longer than the holiday, but they are traditional and lovely with simple ribbons or decorations like cones and berries. And wreaths are also no longer restricted to the front door. Although they make lovely outside decorations, wreaths have been invited indoors and can make a nice wall hanging or even a table centerpiece.

Other Religious Holidays

Religious holidays typically have their preordained decorative items, but there's room for you to stretch your imagination as well. A recent browse through a handblown glass shop revealed unusual menorahs to hold the eight Hanukkah candles. These lovely, traditional candelabra were a design of clear, black, and white glass in geometric patterns that created an architectural feel. Very different!

Cookie-dough ornaments are made from dough comprised of salt and flour and water. There are many recipes available, but basically 4 cups of flour, 1 cup of salt, and around 1½ cups of water will knead up into a good dough. Use cookie cutters to make the shapes you want, and use a toothpick or a straw to make a hole at the top where you can thread string to hang your finished ornament. Bake at 325 degrees until the cookie is hard (as much as one hour). Then paint and decorate as you wish. Spray with varnish to keep them year after year.

Easter-egg painting has gone from the simple kits with plain colors for dying to works of art with kits for intricate Russian-style egg painting and even the use of sequins, braid, and other trim and crafts items. Bunnies and chicks are perennial favorite Easter themes that take the holiday beyond (or away from) its strictly religious founding.

Kid-Oriented Holidays

Kids make holiday decorating great fun. You can add a kid flair to any holiday with paper cutout hearts, pumpkins, shamrocks, trees.

The most flamboyant of all the kid holidays is, of course, Halloween. Draping spider-webs-from-a-can, hanging bats, and finding black cat figurines to skulk around can give a room the creepy air that kids love about this holiday.

Halloween decorating isn't complete until the pumpkins are carved. Although the gap-toothed grin is a classic favorite, pumpkins can take on a whole new look. Kits are readily available with templates designed to make carving unusual faces easy. The pumpkins themselves have been updated. They now come in lots of different shapes and sizes, and even white pumpkins are now readily available. Stack them, scatter them, mount an impressively huge one in a prominent spot, and make Halloween come alive.

Get the kids involved in making the decorations, and you have an automatic popular after-school crafts project. Have things laid out before they get home and they will be able to dive right into making decorations, with time to clean up before supper.

And, speaking of school, oftentimes kids make items in school to celebrate the holidays. Use these in your decorating schemes, especially for those very kid-oriented holidays.

Patriotic Holidays

Patriotic holidays like Memorial Day, Independence Day, and Veteran's Day can be appropriately appointed with simply a showing of the flag. But you don't have to just stick with the plain old red, white, and blue. Many home stores and catalogs are offering old-fashioned flags with a tea-stained appearance so that the white is more off-white and the red is less brilliant. You can get these with the fifty stars or with a circle of stars to represent the thirteen colonies. These old-fashioned flags go very well with the style of an older home. Or you can even get a flag windsock.

If part of your holiday decorating includes hanging an American flag, be sure to follow proper protocol. If you're hanging the flag on a wall or against a building, the field of stars should hang in the upper left. If you hang an American flag on a flagpole with another flag, always be sure the American flag is at the top.

If you want an extremely patriotic décor, bring the red, white, and blue theme into the interior of your home. Hang a smaller flag on a large expanse of wall. Cover some throw pillows with flag-inspired coverings. Display red, white, and blue candles nestled together.

Using Color as a Theme

Although not often thought of in this way, color itself can become a theme. A color as striking as orange or purple can pull together the most everyday items. Pottery pieces, scatter rugs, coasters, and other small pieces can allow you to make color a theme without committing the entire room. It can be great fun searching for items in secondhand and antique stores that fit your color theme.

Perhaps the room itself is the theme color. Say your dining room walls are yellow. Let yellow become a perfect backdrop to white accessories like a tablecloth, white candles in wall sconces, or white drapes with a touch of yellow trim.

In the opposite direction, if your walls are white, liven the room up with accessories of a color theme. It doesn't have to be just at the holidays. With white walls, you can change the color scheme to suit your mood, to suit the season, or to commemorate a holiday if you wish. Warm up a white room in winter with deep burgundy throw pillows and lap blankets, a dark red Persian rug, and furniture slipcovers.

Seasonal Themes

The seasons make dramatic focal points for decorations. You can pull off a big switch by decorating for a season in the opposite season. Do you long for summer in the midst of winter? Hang pictures of summer scenes in prominent places, buy high-quality silk flowers that remind you of the warmer months, and drape your favorite bathing suit and sun hat over the back of the chair in the bedroom or bathroom. This will put you right back on the beach even when the snow is falling outside the window!

If you are more traditional, you will decorate within the season at hand. Of course, this is different for different parts of the country. Decorations for winter in New England might include old wooden ski poles, antique snowshoes, or mittens hand-knit in patterns too elaborate to wear and better enjoyed permanently strung above the woodstove.

FACT

If you can't find just the right tablecloth in the color or pattern that you want, simply go to a good fabric store with a wide selection, buy a few yards of a great fabric, and stitch seams all around to create polished edges. For fabric that is rather thin, line it with a smaller tablecloth or a liner made specifically to go under tablecloths.

Sometimes the seasons naturally bring your home decorations with them. In the fall, the best way to dry bunches of herbs is to hang them from your ceiling beams, at the same time creating a natural décor. The antique umbrella rack that is relegated to the hall closet in the dry summer months may hold a prominent spot in the hall itself during a winter rainy season.

Other Ideas

Do you have a staircase that is open on one side with a wall on the other side that's just begging for some decoration? Collect pictures of dogs or horses or floral paintings and cover the wall with them. Whimsical animals in an array of different frames will have guests lingering on the stairs.

Braided rugs in different colors throughout the house can create a theme on the floor. They don't need to be antiques. There are several companies these days still making quality factory-made braided rugs.

If you really want to go for the theme decoration, fill your house full of 1960s-style furniture and lava lamps, or create a 1950s-style drive-up restaurant theme with car seats for chairs.

Chapter 23

Decorating with Art

Art is essential to good decorating. Whether it is fine art in the form of paintings, sculptures, and photographs, or decorative art such as pottery, glass, and woodwork, art in a style you enjoy makes you feel good simply by being there for you to look at it. It also gives your decorating a totally distinct stamp that is all your own.

What Is Fine Art?

Fine art describes those pieces that are made for art's sake. They don't have an "intended purpose" the way pottery or weaving do. Instead, they are created just for the pleasure of the observer. The two most common fine art pieces the typical homeowner collects are probably paintings and photographs.

You don't have to have lots of discretionary income to start collecting a few pieces of fine art. If you find an original contemporary painting that you would absolutely love to own, many galleries will let you put a deposit on it and pay it off over a certain amount of time. If the gallery is not in your hometown or within driving distance, but instead one you browsed in while on vacation, galleries know how to ship art carefully.

Paintings

Original paintings in either oil, acrylic, or watercolor can be fun and rewarding to decorate your home with. "Original" doesn't mean "old." Buying original works by contemporary artists is a great way to support your local arts community and to decorate your home with unique pieces that suit your style.

ESSENTIAL

There are thousands of art galleries throughout the country that showcase original paintings by local artists. You can find them online with any of the Yellow Pages-type search engines simply by entering a specific Zip Code.

You should hang your paintings with care and learn how to best preserve their original quality. The most important thing is to hang them out of the direct sunlight. Choose a room or a wall that is in the shade all day and shine a light on it that is made for showcasing art. What a great way to brighten up a dark place anyway! Sunlight will not only fade the colors of paintings, fabric, and photographs, but heat from the sun can damage the art as well.

If your painting is extra large, bold in style, or sports an elaborate frame, it will be the focal point for the room you choose to hang it in. Make sure the rest of the room's décor doesn't compete with the painting but instead enhances and even draws attention to it.

Although buying original paintings can cost you a fair amount in some cases, buying original art certainly is not just a pastime for the rich. If you aren't hooked on a specific painting, you can shop around to find something in your price range. The supply is seemingly endless, so if you are patient and persistent, you will find a painting you love and can enjoy the rest of your life.

Photographs

High-quality photographs by professional photographers can make stunning art collections. Though they range in size, on average they are smaller than paintings. A collection of great photographs makes a hallway or a stairwell infinitely more interesting. These are great places to display photos as well since they tend to be windowless areas and there is no sunlight to damage the photos.

E ALERT!

Matting is an essential part of framing a photograph. It's not just for looks. The mat keeps the photograph from touching the glass. Over time a photograph can stick to glass if it is placed against it, ruining the emulsion on the paper and therefore the image.

Photographs by professionals on display in a gallery will most likely be already framed when you purchase them. If not, plan to bring your find to a frame shop and have it professionally framed before you ever bring it home. That way it is ready to hang when it gets to your house. While the frame you choose should certainly have some connection to the décor of the room it will hang in, frames for artworks should always be selected by the needs of the piece of art first, and the room second.

Unless they are old photographs or replicas of old photo techniques, photos are best framed in simple frames with simple matting. The matting can pick up a color in the photo that you would like to enhance or that is in your room. A good framer will be able to walk you through this important process. Framing is a significant expense and a significant addition to the style of the piece, so choose carefully.

Sculpture

Sculpture is perhaps the most interesting art form you can collect for decorating your home. This three-dimensional art form offers great relief from the typically flat surfaces that comprise most of a room. Sculpture is not as common as paintings, photographs, and pencil sketches.

You don't want to make your life miserable trying not to knock it over if your lifestyle is not conducive to keeping a sculpture safe. The heavier materials like bronze or even concrete often are intended to stand on the floor. Sculpture of weather-proof materials make great yard ornamentation as well.

Posters

Posters are not pieces of art in themselves, but they are a great way to enjoy an original from one of the masters or an amazing photo like those of Ansel Adams that would otherwise be unaffordable. Posters are typically quite large and can be very dramatic. They are a bit costly to frame, but the frames can sometimes be reused when you tire of a poster and want to change it.

Fabric Art

Textiles have long been a medium for artists. Fabric art pieces are a unique and vibrant way to decorate a room. Wall hangings in the form of weavings and tapestries bring instant warmth to a room.

It is important to learn how to care for textile pieces. The artist will be able to tell you some cleaning techniques. And, again, the sun is no friend to textile art.

Another way to decorate with textiles in mind is to decorate with the paraphernalia that was part of the textile industry—looms, spinning wheels, spindles, and wood "niddy noddies" (used in making yarn skeins) are all lovely decorative items themselves.

Glass and Ceramics

Hand-blown glass can provide some bold pieces of contemporary art to your home. Pieces are often made to hang in the window, where the sun becomes an artist in helping create the final impact of a piece. Collecting artistically designed vases and platters can also bring art with a function into your home.

As with fine sculpture, if you have small children or rambunctious pets, you may want to avoid tormenting yourself trying to keep these pieces intact. At the very least, have a specific place to display your hand-blown glass treasure that keeps it safe.

FACT

For a glimpse of some unusual textile art, check out the Web site of fabric artist Susan Carlson at ✍ *www.susancarlson.com*. The site shows great photos of her quilts and unique fabric collages that she has done as commissions and tells about her book *Free-Style Quilts: A No-Rules Approach* in which she makes it easy to create your own piece of fabric art.

Folk Art

Folk art takes any number of forms, such as painting on tin, painting on or otherwise decorating utilitarian items, making a funky table out of tobacco tins, or painting the American flag on the side of a barn. Folk art is a strong collectible item. You can learn a lot about folk art at the museum dedicated to it. If you have a chance, visit the Museum of American Folk Art (in New York City, telephone number ✆(212) 595-9533).

Wall Murals

Back in the days before wallpaper was available or easy to get, artists roamed the countryside selling their talents. In exchange for room, board, and perhaps a little cash if possible, they brightened up homes with wall murals. Many of these murals still exist today, sometimes found under layers of wallpaper which, if carefully removed, may have preserved the old murals well. Contemporary artists are reproducing the styles—often considered "primitive"—and technique of the early muralists.

You don't have to keep in the style of that period. If you want to decorate your home with a mural, you can choose any style of painting you like. Of course, the biggest thing you need to keep in mind is that some day you may move and the very nature of a mural, which is painted directly on the wall, means you will have to leave your artwork behind with the new owners.

FACT

Feng shui can be considered when it comes to art in your home. If you want to emphasize a certain element of the Ba-Gua, you can help activate that element with a painting of something appropriate in the corresponding compass direction in a room of your home, say a painting of trees in the east, or "wood," direction of your home.

Trompe L'Oeil

French for "trick the eye," trompe l'oeil is another type of mural, typically painted directly on the wall or perhaps a door. This mural, however, is intended to be realistic and deceive the eye into thinking it sees something that is not really there.

In a windowless room, this may be a window painted on the wall showing blue sky beyond. The window frame might perhaps show some chipping paint, ripples in the panes of glass, and there might be a tree in the distance, maybe even clouds and a bird flying by. You could hang a rolling shade or even curtains and cover the sunny window at night. Or you could paint a rolling shade with a night scene that rolled down at the appropriate time of day.

◀ A fireplace and its mantel make a great place to display a collection of your favorite art pieces.

In the country, a trompe l'oeil could depict an ocean scene or vice versa. Your child's favorite picture book come to life in his or her bedroom is great fun. A popular trend has been to paint a night sky scene on the ceiling, complete with glow-in-the-dark stars and planets available at any nature store.

If you are at all interested in painting, you could attempt a mural or trompe l'oeil yourself. Spend a lot of time sketching your chosen design. Prepare the walls so they are smooth, and paint a plain base color on it. Take some painting classes if it makes you more comfortable putting that brush to the wall.

If you are not artistically inclined, choose a small wall so you won't overwhelm yourself with this big expanse to design and paint. Instead of a small wall, you may want to do something even smaller like a fireplace cover or a door.

Preserving Art

You don't want to purchase a piece of art you adore and not be diligent in its care. The Library of Congress provides information on caring for, cleaning, and preserving art collections of almost any kind through various sections on its Web site (✍ *www.loc.gov*) as well as through its always popular Frequently Asked Questions section. You can contact an expert by writing ✉ Preservation Directorate, Library of Congress, 101 Independence Ave., Washington, D.C., 20540-4500. Their telephone number is ✆ (202) 707-5213, and you can fax them at ✆ (202) 707-3434. E-mail the directorate at *preserve@loc.gov*.

Another online site on art care is the American Institute for Conservation of Historic and Artistic Works. The two sections of particular interest are Caring for Your Treasures, which covers all sorts of materials (ceramic and glass objects, furniture, metal, paintings, photographs, art on paper, and textiles). The other section of interest to home decorators is on disaster recovery, which discusses flooding and other unfortunate incidents. The address for the Institute is ✉ 1717 K Street, NW, Suite 200, Washington, D.C., 20006. Their great Web site is located at ✍ *www.aic.stanford.edu*. Ⓔ

Chapter 24

Apartment Decorating

Apartments often have unique decorating considerations. You can follow the same decorating rules of thumb that you would if you were decorating a multiroom house. But you may have fewer rooms, less space, and little storage in an apartment. You may also not want to spend much money on improvements that will be left behind when your lease is up and you move.

Size Concerns

Apartments can be as large in square feet as an average house. Or they can be as small in square feet as an average room in an average house. If the latter is the case for your apartment, you will have some unique decorating challenges.

Don't make a small apartment seem smaller by crowding it full of stuff. Use the same techniques described in previous chapters to make ceilings look higher and rooms look larger. Use light colors on the walls to make the space feel bigger, or at least not smaller.

If you need to transform a living room into a bedroom every day by pulling out a sleep sofa, be sure you either decorate so that you don't need to move other stuff each night, or make sure they are easy to move. Don't stack a coffee table with heavy magazines that make the coffee table difficult to lift. Design the decorating of the room around this important space-conserving need.

Use wall space for things that can hang instead of taking up precious floor space. Make sure to maximize what cupboard and closet space you have.

ESSENTIAL

Check out hotels and mobile homes if you want to see space maximized. But you don't need to make your apartment look like a hotel in order to make use of the ideas you find. Things like retractable clotheslines that hang in the bathtub and folding racks for suitcases can be adapted to many possibilities. Small refrigerators and under-the-counter appliances that hang from the upper cupboard to free up counter space are just a small sampling of possibilities.

If one room needs to serve several purposes, consider creative use of dressing screens and shoji screens. They can be easily moved if you simply feel the need to open the place up once in a while. Or, if you'd rather the computer desk was more private, turn bookcases so they are perpendicular to the wall and make your own wall space. Put a side table against the open back of the bookcase, put a plant on top of the table, and you'll hardly notice that you are looking at the back of a piece of furniture, especially if you are careful to choose a bookcase that has a finished back.

When choosing furniture, space considerations will likely be your top priority. First, think foldable, rollable, nesting, or anything else that will easily reduce in size when not in use.

Folding Furniture

Folding chairs designed for outdoor furniture or card table use can make comfortable dining chairs. If you have enough space, get a more substantial dining chair for the number of occupants in the apartment (probably not more than two for this size apartment anyway) and tuck a couple of folding chairs away in a closet or behind a door for use when guests come. A card table itself could even serve as a dining table. Put an elegant tablecloth on it, and who would know or care what's underneath?

Install an ironing board that folds up against the inside of a closet door where it is hidden out of sight and, more importantly, out of the way. Buy a cabinet for the television and other electronic equipment to be able to store them all in one small space, and shut the doors when you aren't watching television. If you can afford the slightly greater cost, buy a cabinet with pocket doors that slide back into the cabinet when it's open rather than those that swing out and take up space.

Rolling Furniture

Furniture on wheels can be rolled out of the way when more space is needed. Rolling butcher blocks can provide the extra counter space near the stove, and you can roll them back over by the back door when you are done cooking. When you need to move things around a lot, wheels make the job a lot easier. Wheels also come in handy when you are organizing the kitchen cupboards. Use things that roll easily and smoothly

◀ In a bathroom where storage space is minimal, look for creative ways to make your own space. If your sink is not placed in a cabinet top, you can still create room for storage below it by adding a fabric curtain around the sink.

out from the back of the cupboard so you don't have to miss all the extra cupboard space you might have in a larger place.

Look at other rolling pieces and consider what else they could be used for. Just because a computer stand is designed for a computer doesn't mean it has to be relegated only to housing a computer. Maybe it's the perfect item to hold the supplies for a craft you are involved in— the computer stand has several shelves that can hold many containers of beads or lace or whatever you like. The keyboard shelf can hold a tray with pins, scissors, tape measure, and other small supplies that can simply roll back out of the way. Think beyond the usual.

Rolling of a different sort is exemplified by the roll-top desk. This or a desk with a fold-down writing table can give you the room you need to spread out a little and do bills. At the same time, you can hide everything and reduce your space needs just by rolling or folding the desk surface out of the way. Anything that helps make the room look neat and less full is good in an apartment if space is an issue.

Nesting Furniture

Nesting things allow for several items to take up only one footprint of floor space. Stacking chairs can hide in a closet. Nesting end tables are very traditional. Three tables, each one smaller than the main one, tuck into each other and can be pulled out for company or when you need a little extra space for knitting items or a coffee cup. You don't need to have an end table at every chair when you only use one most often. Instead, just pull each table out when you need it. A trundle bed is another kind of nesting furniture—a guest bed that rolls under a daybed or your main bed. These were common in Colonial times, but you can still easily find them today in contemporary furniture styles.

ALERT!

Begin collecting great pieces of furniture while you are still in a small apartment. A dining room table is always a good purchase and can be used for many different tasks besides dining. You don't have to wait until you're staring at the blank walls of your newly purchased home to collect fine furniture and interesting decorative pieces.

The Temporary Home

Temporary doesn't have to refer just to a place you rented for a few weeks while you found a new house. Temporary may mean several years. The point is that you don't own the place and you will likely someday move to another place.

You probably won't want to do things like stencil walls and floors in a place you are going to leave behind in less than ten years or so—your landlord may not appreciate it anyway. If you just like to stencil and the landlord doesn't mind, then by all means, stencil away. But there are faster and easier ways to achieve the look of stenciling without spending hours and hours on it. Less time-consuming and heartbreaking to leave behind would be a wallpaper border. Or, if you would love to stencil the floor, consider making a floor cloth and stenciling it—you can simply roll that up and take it along at a moment's notice.

Don't install your favorite handmade ceramic tiles across the back of the sink as a backsplash in the kitchen and have to say goodbye to them two years later. Just lean them up against the backsplash, enjoy them, and take them to your new home when you move.

Same with pictures. If your landlord limits the number of holes you can pound in the wall, you can find other ways to decorate. Instead of hanging pictures, buy small frames that can stand up on a shelf, or lean them against the back of a bookshelf. Use mirrors that have their own pedestal.

If you really need lots of hooks to hang things from—pots and pans, jackets, hats, or cleaning supplies—don't hang a separate hook for each thing. Instead, hang a series of hooks attached to a backing that only needs two screws to mount. Perhaps you feel that cramps your style when it comes to making your own pegs out of bent spoons, old horseshoes, drawer knobs, or old cane or umbrella handles. You can still make your own pegs but again, mount them to a board and hang that board with just a couple of screws. Not only does it save the wall and keep your landlord happy, but it's easier to take with you when you move.

The Upper Floor Apartment

If you live in a tall apartment building where many of the apartments are on the interior of the building and on floors fifteen or twenty stories up, the building will almost certainly have a freight elevator for use by tenants. With a freight elevator, moving furniture to your apartment shouldn't be a problem.

However, if you are on the third floor of a four- or five-story walk-up, you will want to choose your furniture according to the number of strong friends and family members you have who might be willing to help you move it in—and out again when you move on.

Try to stick with pieces that are easily broken down. This doesn't mean you can't be starting to purchase those antiques you've always wanted to purchase—just start with things like chests of drawers until you are in a different living situation. The drawers can all be moved separately, and the chest won't be unmanageable.

Decorating Rules

Just because your home is an apartment, it doesn't mean that there won't be a focal point to a room around which you can decorate. If you don't plan to be there more than a couple of years, you won't want to buy your furniture, drapes, and other accessories only to take advantage of that specific focal point, but it is rare that that would be necessary.

The same with color scheme. If your landlord won't let you paint the walls the colors you would like or repaint at all, you can use all the decorating tips that we have covered in the past twenty-plus chapters to make the existing color work.

If you include your favorite things in your home, you will feel at home even if you don't own the building! (E)

Chapter 25

Solving Common Problems

Any house, no matter how large or how small, will present you with some decorating problems that must be solved. Either something doesn't fit, clutter gets in your way, or you can't agree on a paint color. But you can be prepared, and preparation will help you confront these issues as creative challenges rather than frustrations.

Getting the Bed Upstairs

Old houses can present a nasty problem. Contemporary furniture sizes are often difficult to get to the second floor! Many houses built before the twentieth century have narrow doorways, staircases, and stairwells that aren't just tight but turn a tight corner. But even if, like one couple, you have to remove the stairwell and rope-and-pulley your current queen-sized mattress and box spring up to the bedroom, don't despair. Times have changed in the mattress business.

Mattress style	Dimensions
Twin	39" x 75"
Long twin	39" x 80"
Full	54" x 75"
Queen	60" x 80"
King	76" x 80"
California King	72" x 84"

The measurements of the standard mattress styles are shown to the left.

A modern mattress can withstand being bent three times in its lifetime. When the bent mattress is set on the box spring, it is set with the bend concave. It will pretty quickly settle into its original position from its own weight and yours.

King size box springs are actually in two pieces, which are two "long" twin size box springs. Those are typically easy to get up most stairwells. And many times now, queen box springs also come as split boxes, making them easier to get up the stairs as well.

ALERT!

Before you go buy a new bed or a significant piece of furniture, you need to be sure that it not only fits in the space you want it to go in, but that it will fit through the doorways, stairwells, and hallways it will have to go through to get there. Measure carefully and have your furnishings store staff help—they have seen almost everything and have great tricks-of-the-trade on how to move things.

Paint Remedies

If you've done your homework and chosen as carefully as you know how, never be afraid to try out a paint color. If you paint the whole wall and when it dries it just doesn't work the way you thought it might, you can always paint over it. But before you do that, maybe instead of painting over it with yet another color you are unsure of, consider doing a faux finish. The color may be the perfect background for sponge painting, marbling, or other faux finishes. They are easy and fun.

You can get all the supplies at your local paint store, along with instructions. Tools now exist to make this kind of handiwork even easier, such as sponge rollers with decorative carving already in them and patterns to follow or use on the wall. It's simple, and the results can look very impressive. You don't want to overdo this kind of paint technique in your home, but definitely give it a try on a small area or when things just aren't working out.

You can also consider a border around the top, a chair rail border, or—if you really want to spend some energy—install a wainscoting around the bottom, a border on the top, and the color that's left showing may be just right!

Disagreements over Decorating

There are probably going to be times when you and your spouse can't seem to agree on some major decorating decisions that you need to make for your home. This can be a difficult situation, but before you end up with something that neither of you really likes, make sure your decision-making is coming from a logical place to begin with.

Go through the list of questions that need to be answered when working with any room in your home:

- What is the main use of this room?
- What are the one or two significant secondary uses of this room (that is, things the room is used for more than once a year)?
- What kind of atmosphere should this room represent? Warm, cool, relaxing, inspiring, invigorating? (This will help narrow color choices down to a select two or three.)
- What kind of furniture is practical for the main function of the room?

271

- What kind of furniture will be wanted for secondary uses of the room?
- Is there a way you can easily try each of the ideas for decorating the room without more than a couple of hours work?

Don't paint walls or floors, wallpaper, or do any of the more "permanent" things, but do rearrange the furniture, pull in some pieces from other rooms, and use temporary slipcovers (like sheets and blankets) that resemble the ultimate color scheme. Live with each for a month or so and see how you feel. Make notes at the end of each decorating scheme's trial period, and you may be surprised at the final decisions you can make! For a decorating scheme that you would like to last five or ten years, a little extra time to make good decisions and make everyone happy is definitely worthwhile.

FACT

Couples in disagreement about design and decorating issues are such a common problem that Home and Garden TV (HGTV) has created a whole show called *Battle of the Sexes*. The show's host, a professional interior designer, interviews couples about the particular issue they are trying to solve, tours the home and the specific room, takes them (and viewers) on a shopping trip to pick out materials, fixtures, and furnishings, and then gives us a glimpse of the finished room and the happy couple!

Keeping Clear of Clutter

Do you get frustrated by the clutter that seems to ruin all the good decorating work you've done? Small houses and apartments are particularly susceptible, but any home can be taken over by clutter.

The key to tackling clutter is to have a place for everything. That way, even if the newspaper always ends up on the living room floor, it's easy for anyone in the household to pick it up on their way out of the room and deposit it in the easily accessible recycling bin.

Sort through junk mail immediately, before the mail even reaches the kitchen counter or dining room table. Throw away anything that you absolutely know you are not interested in. Keep an envelope opener handy and make it easy to sort through the mail. Have a place for bills to go so you can immediately put those there once the appropriate family members have had a chance to see the day's mail. Magazine racks can be bought to go with any decorating style—buy one big enough for the number of subscriptions you have coming into the house. Do you really need to keep those old issues? If so, get a heavy-duty hole punch and enough ring binders or magazine holders for each subscription, and store them neatly in their own container on a bookshelf.

Give a careful look at what actually constitutes clutter in your house, and begin to create space for these items. Closet storage organizers, drawer organizers, and any manner of cubicle and plastic containers will help you get the clutter out of view.

Mural under Wallpaper

You went to redecorate your nineteenth-century home, and when you started to pull the wallpaper off the living room walls, you found that at some point in your house's history there was a mural painted on the wall. What do you do now?

First, contact the local historical society. If there isn't one in your town, find one in a neighboring town. They will be able to help you determine whether there are historical records of an itinerant muralist that traveled through your town, which might help determine whether your mural may be of historical significance. They can also help you find out if there are any other murals in buildings in your town or neighboring towns that might help you determine who painted yours.

Historical societies will be able to direct you to local resources—both information and perhaps financial—that will be able to help you preserve as much of the mural as possible in the wallpaper-removal process and to help preserve or restore the original mural if it is found to have historical value. When you purchase and redecorate an older home, always be on the lookout for this kind of hidden authentic detail. Don't be in such a hurry to get the room redecorated that you don't want to stop and take the time to preserve things. Your home will be more valuable for it, and you will be helping to keep a part of our past intact.

Unfinished Business and Contractors

You thought you were doing the right thing hiring a contractor to do a substantial and complicated painting job for your living room and dining room. She came on time, got partway done, but now you haven't seen her for several weeks.

The first thing you need to consider is whether or not there is a written contract that you can fall back on. To be helpful, the contract will need to have the details of not only what is going to be done to the room(s) but what the timeframe is for completion, including all the last details. You should never hire a professional decorator or contractor without a formal, written contract estimating cost, time, and what happens if these two don't work out as contracted.

ALERT!

Always get a written contract from any professional you hire to do work in your home for more than $100. The contract should outline more than just what the job will cost. Be sure it states a completion date and what happens if the job is shaping up to cost more than 10 percent over the estimate.

If the contractor is part of a bigger company, use the "squeaky wheel gets the grease" approach. Call them frequently. Make it clear that you expect their person to do the job professionally as contracted. If the contractor is an independent, that won't be as easy. You may get their answering machine or even them saying that they will come back, but actually getting them there is a different story.

To avoid this, besides researching their reputation up front, you should also only pay your contractors a portion of the job before they get started. If they disappear and won't respond to your concerns, find someone else to finish it up. You may be out a few bucks, but you're not taking as much risk if you only pay in predetermined increments based strictly on work completed.

Creating a "Fireplace" Without One

Maybe you like the look of a fireplace but you live in an apartment that doesn't have a fireplace, and you are probably going to move inside of three years anyway.

If you'd like to enjoy the look of a fireplace in the meantime, shop at one of the architectural salvage yards or in some of the more substantial furnishings catalogs and buy a mantel. You will need a room with an open wall space to install the mantel, but you can then have a lot of fun with a decorative fire—either paint it in trompe l'oeil style or build it out a little from the wall, put a grate on the floor and stack some wood in it, or actually create a "fire" out of decorative lighting. And you can take the mantel with you when you go!

Inheriting Family Heirlooms

Your parents have sold the family homestead and after a long decision-making process are finally moving into that smaller home. They want to give you that massive hutch or desk or some other huge family heirloom that, every time you look at it, makes you recall fond memories of your childhood. It's a fine, valuable, sentimental piece, but in your home would be a monstrosity. What do you do?

Consider storing it for a while. Find a storage facility that can guarantee that it is stored in the best climate and conditions for the piece, and sit on it for as much as ten years if you can. Storage facilities aren't that expensive. Don't give up on the piece yet. You may think now that you are never going to move, but in ten years any number of things may have changed to make you decide to move into a home that the piece might fit into. Or maybe children will be grown by then and be in a position to take the piece. If it is really a valuable piece with some history, you could also consider donating it to the local historical museum or lending it to a historical home with the idea that you may take it back someday for personal use.

Sticking to a Small Budget

You love to decorate but you can't afford to change things and add things as often as you would like. There are lots of ways to decorate inexpensively. Do you really need antiques? Maybe "secondhand" would serve your purposes just as well for a lot less money.

If you don't have a lot of discretionary income to spend on decorating, but you would love to redecorate rooms more regularly, get creative! Arrange with a few friends to hold a "decorating swap" once or twice a year. Everyone has yards of fabric they just had to have that ends up sitting in boxes in the closet. Maybe someone tried quilting once and has no plans to ever quilt again—instead of spending $100 on basic quilting supplies, you could swap for your friend's or buy them from her cheaply. Maybe that stool you always thought you would refinish has sat in the attic long enough, and one of your swap-mates would love to try decoupage with it. You could get redecorating ideas and supplies cheaply and have fun too!

Are there things around your home that you could use differently? Haul something out of the closet, and re-examine the attic on a regular basis. You'd be surprised what you forgot about.

Exchange stuff with other people. Have a decorating swap.

Learn to make things yourself. There is no end to the opportunities to learn a craft that will provide you with endless, inexpensive decorating items. If you don't want to spend the money on classes, this category is usually well stocked in even the smallest of libraries. Or check out videos or television crafts shows like Carol Duvall on HGTV—for a list of upcoming shows, search the HGTV Web site at *www.hgtv.com*—where in one week you can learn how to make anything from beaded flowers to floor pillows to felted wall sculptures and tons more besides.

Problems are only problems if you approach them with the wrong attitude. Look at problems as fun decorating challenges, and you will be on your way to solving almost any problem you encounter! Ⓔ

Appendices

Appendix A
Resources

Appendix B

Glossary

Resources

There are many books and magazines available that can help you with more great ideas for decorating your home. Here's a list of some good places to begin your search for the perfect touches for your home.

Books

Interior Design on Your Own by Jill Blake, Consumer Reports Books, 1986.

Nina Campbell's Decorating Secrets by Helen Chislett, Clarkson Potter, 2000.

The Simon and Schuster Complete Guide to Home Repair and Maintenance, by Bernard Gladstone, Simon and Schuster, 1984.

Feng Shui: Arranging Your Home to Change Your Life, by Kirsten M. Lagatree, Villard, 1996.

The Healthy Living Space, by Richard Leviton, Hampton Roads Publishing Company, 2001.

50 Favorite Rooms by Frank Lloyd Wright, by Diane Maddex, Smithmark, 1998.

House Comfortable, by Katharine Kaye McMillan and Patricia Hart McMillan, Perigee, 1996.

Home Comforts: The Art & Science of Keeping House, by Cheryl Mendelson, Scribner, 1999.

Perfect Country Rooms, by Emma-Louise O'Reilly, Abbeville, 1996.

Outdoor Living with Style, by Ellen M. Plante, Friedman/Fairfax, 1999.

Feng Shui: The Chinese Art of Placement, by Sarah Rossbach, Penguin, 1983.

Living Color: Master Lin Yun's Guide to Feng Shui and the Art of Color, Sarah Rossbach and Lin Yun, Kodansha, 1994.

The Ultimate Home Style Guide, by Katherine Sorrell, Ward Lock, 1998.

The Decoration of Houses, by Alexandra Stoddard, Avon, 1997.

The Lighting Book: A Complete Guide to Lighting Your Home, by Deyan Sudjic, Crown, 1985.

Ideas for Great Window Treatments, Sunset, 1992.

Use What You Have Decorating, by Lauri Ward, G. P. Putnam's Sons, 1998.

Magazines

Better Homes and Gardens
Coastal Living
Country Living
Creative Home
Decorating Ideas
Elle Décor
House Beautiful
Metropolitan Home
Mountain Living
Natural Home
Southern Accents
Traditional Home
Victorian Homes

Appendix B

Glossary

From "Ba-Gua" to "vernacular": all the words you need to know to navigate the world of home décor. This glossary will help you make sense of the jargon.

Ba-Gua: The energy road map that outlines the elements and is used in practicing feng shui.

bias cut: Cutting fabric diagonally from its weave. Strips cut on the bias are used to edge pillows and create piping.

brocade: A fabric or wallpaper with a raised design.

CAD: Computer-aided design. CAD programs can be used to help with decorating decisions.

ceiling medallion: A centerpiece in the ceiling usually decorating the point at which a chandelier comes out of the ceiling.

chi: The energy that is within us and around us (also "qi").

childproofing: Looking carefully around your home and eliminating situations that are hazardous to children, such as high dressers that could topple on them if they climb them; installing safety wallplates that cover unused outlets.

color wheel: Primary, secondary, and tertiary colors represented on a wheel to show which colors are analogous or complementary to each other.

DIY: Do-it-yourself, a common acronym for homeowners who like to tackle projects in their homes.

drywall: Also called gypsum wallboard or Sheetrock (which is a manufacturer of drywall). Came to almost entirely replace plaster in the latter half of the twentieth century for wall and ceiling surfaces.

eclectic: Taking what you like from many styles and combining them in one room or home.

fenestration: The collective arrangement of windows in a room or house.

finial: A crowning ornament or detail (as on a piece of furniture).

fluorescent lighting: Lighting that is produced by the excitation of fluorescent phosphorus by ultraviolet radiation.

frieze: A decorative element along the upper edge of a wall, often an ongoing scene either painted on or depicted with a wallpaper border.

gazebo: A freestanding outdoor structure with a roof, sometimes with screened sides. Usually octagon shaped but it can be square as well.

gold leaf: A process by which thin sheets, or "leaves," of gold are used to decorate.

halogen lighting: Lights that are produced by halogen gas heating up a metal wire to a high intensity.

illuminance: How much light falls on a surface. Measured in lumens per square foot.

incandescent light: A bulb that has a filament that produces light when it is heated to a certain point.

indirect lighting: Lighting that reflects off a surface such as a wall or ceiling, with the rest of the light shining into the room.

linoleum: A flooring made of oxidized linseed oil which is mixed with cork or "wood flour," mineral filler, and pigments to create color, all bonded to a backing which is often jute.

pile: The depth of the plushness of a carpet. For example, indoor/outdoor carpeting is a low pile carpet, while the classic 1970s shag rug was a very deep pile carpet.

primer paint: Typically in a flat white color, this paint prepares the surface for the finish coats of paint by sealing porous new material or helping cover dark colors before the top coat or two is painted on.

refacing: Keeping the original structure and resurfacing, such as leaving the basic structure of kitchen cabinets, recovering their surface with a veneer, and putting on new doors and drawers.

reflector lamp: A lamp that has a reflecting surface as a part of the lamp. Some lamps can have reflectors added to them.

repeats: When choosing wallpaper with a pattern, the book will tell how many vertical inches the pattern goes before it repeats. A shorter repeat means you will waste less wallpaper matching the pattern on walls that have lots of doorways and architectural details that require short lengths of wallpaper.

scatter rugs: Also called throw rugs, these are small rugs intended to have a specific purpose such as for wiping shoes before entering the house, covering a seam in linoleum, softening the floor where you stand for long periods such as at a sink or stove, or simply adding nice color to a room.

Stickley: Designer of Arts & Crafts style furnishings. Reproduction lines of Stickley furniture are still available using Stickley's original blueprints for his designs.

task lighting: Lighting directed toward a specific location to illuminate a particular activity such as reading or bill paying.

veneer: Laying a more expensive wood on a base of a less expensive, more common wood.

vernacular: Of, relating to, or characteristic of a certain period or place.

Index

THE EVERYTHING SERIES!

BUSINESS

Everything® Business Planning Book
Everything® Coaching and Mentoring Book
Everything® Fundraising Book
Everything® Home-Based Business Book
Everything® Landlording Book
Everything® Leadership Book
Everything® Managing People Book
Everything® Negotiating Book
Everything® Network Marketing Book
Everything® Online Business Book
Everything® Project Management Book
Everything® Robert's Rules Book,
    $7.95($11.95 CAN)
Everything® Selling Book
Everything® Start Your Own Business Book
Everything® Time Management Book

COMPUTERS

Everything® Build Your Own Home Page Book
Everything® Computer Book

COOKBOOKS

Everything® Barbecue Cookbook
Everything® Bartender's Book, $9.95
    ($15.95 CAN)
Everything® Chinese Cookbook
Everything® Chocolate Cookbook
Everything® Cookbook
Everything® Dessert Cookbook
Everything® Diabetes Cookbook
Everything® Fondue Cookbook
Everything® Grilling Cookbook
Everything® Holiday Cookbook
Everything® Indian Cookbook
Everything® Low-Carb Cookbook
Everything® Low-Fat High-Flavor Cookbook
Everything® Low-Salt Cookbook
Everything® Mediterranean Cookbook
Everything® Mexican Cookbook
Everything® One-Pot Cookbook

Everything® Pasta Cookbook
Everything® Quick Meals Cookbook
Everything® Slow Cooker Cookbook
Everything® Soup Cookbook
Everything® Thai Cookbook
Everything® Vegetarian Cookbook
Everything® Wine Book

HEALTH

Everything® Alzheimer's Book
Everything® Anti-Aging Book
Everything® Diabetes Book
Everything® Dieting Book
Everything® Hypnosis Book
Everything® Low Cholesterol Book
Everything® Massage Book
Everything® Menopause Book
Everything® Nutrition Book
Everything® Reflexology Book
Everything® Reiki Book
Everything® Stress Management Book
Everything® Vitamins, Minerals, and
    Nutritional Supplements Book

HISTORY

Everything® American Government Book
Everything® American History Book
Everything® Civil War Book
Everything® Irish History & Heritage Book
Everything® Mafia Book
Everything® Middle East Book

HOBBIES & GAMES

Everything® Bridge Book
Everything® Candlemaking Book
Everything® Card Games Book
Everything® Cartooning Book
Everything® Casino Gambling Book, 2nd Ed.
Everything® Chess Basics Book
Everything® Collectibles Book
Everything® Crossword and Puzzle Book

Everything® Crossword Challenge Book
Everything® Drawing Book
Everything® Digital Photography Book
Everything® Easy Crosswords Book
Everything® Family Tree Book
Everything® Games Book
Everything® Knitting Book
Everything® Magic Book
Everything® Motorcycle Book
Everything® Online Genealogy Book
Everything® Photography Book
Everything® Poker Strategy Book
Everything® Pool & Billiards Book
Everything® Quilting Book
Everything® Scrapbooking Book
Everything® Sewing Book
Everything® Soapmaking Book

HOME IMPROVEMENT

Everything® Feng Shui Book
Everything® Feng Shui Decluttering Book,
    $9.95 ($15.95 CAN)
Everything® Fix-It Book
Everything® Homebuilding Book
Everything® Home Decorating Book
Everything® Landscaping Book
Everything® Lawn Care Book
Everything® Organize Your Home Book

EVERYTHING® KIDS' BOOKS

All titles are $6.95 ($10.95 Canada)
unless otherwise noted
Everything® Kids' Baseball Book, 3rd Ed.
Everything® Kids' Bible Trivia Book
Everything® Kids' Bugs Book
Everything® Kids' Christmas Puzzle
    & Activity Book
Everything® Kids' Cookbook
Everything® Kids' Halloween Puzzle
    & Activity Book ($9.95 CAN)

All Everything® books are priced at $12.95 or $14.95, unless otherwise stated. Prices subject to change without notice.
Canadian prices range from $11.95–$31.95, and are subject to change without notice.

Everything® Kids' Hidden Pictures Book
   ($9.95 CAN)
Everything® Kids' Joke Book
Everything® Kids' Knock Knock Book
   ($9.95 CAN)
Everything® Kids' Math Puzzles Book
Everything® Kids' Mazes Book
Everything® Kids' Money Book ($11.95 CAN)
Everything® Kids' Monsters Book
Everything® Kids' Nature Book ($11.95 CAN)
Everything® Kids' Puzzle Book
Everything® Kids' Riddles & Brain Teasers Book
Everything® Kids' Science Experiments Book
Everything® Kids' Soccer Book
Everything® Kids' Travel Activity Book

KIDS' STORY BOOKS

Everything® Bedtime Story Book
Everything® Bible Stories Book
Everything® Fairy Tales Book
Everything® Mother Goose Book

LANGUAGE

Everything® Conversational Japanese Book
   (with CD), $19.95 ($31.95 CAN)
Everything® Inglés Book
Everything® French Phrase Book, $9.95
   ($15.95 CAN)
Everything® Learning French Book
Everything® Learning German Book
Everything® Learning Italian Book
Everything® Learning Latin Book
Everything® Learning Spanish Book
Everything® Sign Language Book
Everything® Spanish Phrase Book,
   $9.95 ($15.95 CAN)
Everything® Spanish Verb Book,
   $9.95 ($15.95 CAN)

MUSIC

Everything® Drums Book (with CD),
   $19.95 ($31.95 CAN)
Everything® Guitar Book
Everything® Home Recording Book
Everything® Playing Piano and Keyboards Book
Everything® Rock & Blues Guitar Book
   (with CD), $19.95 ($31.95 CAN)
Everything® Songwriting Book

NEW AGE

Everything® Astrology Book
Everything® Divining the Future Book
Everything® Dreams Book
Everything® Ghost Book
Everything® Love Signs Book,
   $9.95 ($15.95 CAN)
Everything® Meditation Book
Everything® Numerology Book
Everything® Paganism Book
Everything® Palmistry Book
Everything® Psychic Book
Everything® Spells & Charms Book
Everything® Tarot Book
Everything® Wicca and Witchcraft Book

PARENTING

Everything® Baby Names Book
Everything® Baby Shower Book
Everything® Baby's First Food Book
Everything® Baby's First Year Book
Everything® Birthing Book
Everything® Breastfeeding Book
Everything® Father-to-Be Book
Everything® Get Ready for Baby Book
Everything® Getting Pregnant Book
Everything® Homeschooling Book
Everything® Parent's Guide to Children
   with Asperger's Syndrome
Everything® Parent's Guide to Children
   with Autism
Everything® Parent's Guide to Children
   with Dyslexia
Everything® Parent's Guide to Positive Discipline
Everything® Parent's Guide to Raising a
   Successful Child
Everything® Parenting a Teenager Book
Everything® Potty Training Book,
   $9.95 ($15.95 CAN)
Everything® Pregnancy Book, 2nd Ed.
Everything® Pregnancy Fitness Book
Everything® Pregnancy Nutrition Book
Everything® Pregnancy Organizer,
   $15.00 ($22.95 CAN)
Everything® Toddler Book
Everything® Tween Book

PERSONAL FINANCE

Everything® Budgeting Book
Everything® Get Out of Debt Book

(untitled)

Everything® Get Rich Book
Everything® Homebuying Book, 2nd Ed.
Everything® Homeselling Book
Everything® Investing Book
Everything® Money Book
Everything® Mutual Funds Book
Everything® Online Business Book
Everything® Personal Finance Book
Everything® Personal Finance in Your
   20s & 30s Book
Everything® Real Estate Investing Book
Everything® Wills & Estate Planning Book

PETS

Everything® Cat Book
Everything® Dog Book
Everything® Dog Training and Tricks Book
Everything® Golden Retriever Book
Everything® Horse Book
Everything® Labrador Retriever Book
Everything® Poodle Book
Everything® Puppy Book
Everything® Rottweiler Book
Everything® Tropical Fish Book

REFERENCE

Everything® Astronomy Book
Everything® Car Care Book
Everything® Christmas Book,
   $15.00 ($21.95 CAN)
Everything® Classical Mythology Book
Everything® Einstein Book
Everything® Etiquette Book
Everything® Great Thinkers Book
Everything® Philosophy Book
Everything® Psychology Book
Everything® Shakespeare Book
Everything® Tall Tales, Legends, & Other
   Outrageous Lies Book
Everything® Toasts Book
Everything® Trivia Book
Everything® Weather Book

RELIGION

Everything® Angels Book
Everything® Bible Book
Everything® Buddhism Book
Everything® Catholicism Book
Everything® Christianity Book
Everything® Jewish History & Heritage Book

All Everything® books are priced at $12.95 or $14.95, unless otherwise stated. Prices subject to change without notice.
Canadian prices range from $11.95–$31.95, and are subject to change without notice.

Everything® Judaism Book
Everything® Koran Book
Everything® Prayer Book
Everything® Saints Book
Everything® Understanding Islam Book
Everything® World's Religions Book
Everything® Zen Book

SCHOOL & CAREERS

Everything® After College Book
Everything® Alternative Careers Book
Everything® College Survival Book
Everything® Cover Letter Book
Everything® Get-a-Job Book
Everything® Hot Careers Book
Everything® Job Interview Book
Everything® New Teacher Book
Everything® Online Job Search Book
Everything® Personal Finance Book
Everything® Practice Interview Book
Everything® Resume Book, 2nd Ed.
Everything® Study Book

SELF-HELP/ RELATIONSHIPS

Everything® Dating Book
Everything® Divorce Book
Everything® Great Marriage Book
Everything® Great Sex Book
Everything® Kama Sutra Book
Everything® Romance Book
Everything® Self-Esteem Book
Everything® Success Book

SPORTS & FITNESS

Everything® Body Shaping Book
Everything® Fishing Book
Everything® Fly-Fishing Book
Everything® Golf Book
Everything® Golf Instruction Book
Everything® Knots Book
Everything® Pilates Book
Everything® Running Book
Everything® Sailing Book, 2nd Ed.
Everything® T'ai Chi and QiGong Book
Everything® Total Fitness Book
Everything® Weight Training Book
Everything® Yoga Book

TRAVEL

Everything® Family Guide to Hawaii
Everything® Family Guide to New York City, 2nd Ed.
Everything® Family Guide to Washington D.C., 2nd Ed.
Everything® Family Guide to the Walt Disney World Resort®, Universal Studios®, and Greater Orlando, 4th Ed.
Everything® Guide to Las Vegas
Everything® Guide to New England
Everything® Travel Guide to the Disneyland Resort®, California Adventure®, Universal Studios®, and the Anaheim Area

WEDDINGS

Everything® Bachelorette Party Book, $9.95 ($15.95 CAN)

Everything® Bridesmaid Book, $9.95 ($15.95 CAN)
Everything® Creative Wedding Ideas Book
Everything® Elopement Book, $9.95 ($15.95 CAN)
Everything® Father of the Bride Book, $9.95 ($15.95 CAN)
Everything® Groom Book, $9.95 ($15.95 CAN)
Everything® Jewish Wedding Book
Everything® Mother of the Bride Book, $9.95 ($15.95)
Everything® Wedding Book, 3rd Ed.
Everything® Wedding Checklist, $7.95 ($12.95 CAN)
Everything® Wedding Etiquette Book, $7.95 ($12.95 CAN)
Everything® Wedding Organizer, $15.00 ($22.95 CAN)
Everything® Wedding Shower Book, $7.95 ($12.95 CAN)
Everything® Wedding Vows Book, $7.95 ($12.95 CAN)
Everything® Weddings on a Budget Book, $9.95 ($15.95 CAN)

WRITING

Everything® Creative Writing Book
Everything® Get Published Book
Everything® Grammar and Style Book
Everything® Grant Writing Book
Everything® Guide to Writing a Novel
Everything® Guide to Writing Children's Books
Everything® Screenwriting Book
Everything® Writing Well Book

Introducing an exceptional new line of beginner craft books from the Everything® series!

All titles are $14.95 ($22.95 CAN)

Everything® Crafts—Create Your Own Greeting Cards
1-59337-226-4

Everything® Crafts—Polymer Clay for Beginners
1-59337-230-2

Everything® Crafts—Rubberstamping Made Easy
1-59337-229-9

Everything® Crafts—Wedding Decorations and Keepsakes
1-59337-227-2

Available wherever books are sold!
To order, call 800-872-5627, or visit us at *www.everything.com*
Everything® and everything.com® are registered trademarks of F+W Publications, Inc.